Copyright ©

gr

All rights reserved. No part of this book (including its images may be reproduced or used in any manner without written permission of the copyright owner except for the use of quotations in a review or a short quote for a publication. The moral rights of the author have been asserted.

First paperback edition June 2021

ISBN: 9798512085653

Imprint: Independently published

This book is dedicated to:
First of all my Mum who given the choice I couldn't have chosen better. She was also largely responsible for editing the book.
Juliette (Ferret) my partner of 10 years who has supported me through all my endeavours and mental struggles.
My two daughters Isabella and Sofia who are the greatest things to ever happen to me!
My brother Jamie who apart from his sense of humour has also partnered me in many of my property ventures.
Paps (my Dad) for giving me a leg up when needed and refusing anything in return.
Christina my sister for finding me a great house that my brother and I could renovate and rent to her at practically a loss.
Dean Sanderson my old boss, friend and Mentor.
Walter Dixon who has done many renovations for me but more importantly given me a wealth of building knowledge.
Ciaran Heaney my old neighbour and friend who has worked for me for a pittance.
Karen Lee and Gareth Davenport my financial advisors who have put up with my incessant questions.
Martin Reynolds my father in law (practically) for the odd emergency financial assistance and refusing anything in return.
And last of all anyone else who has helped me along the way.
I THANK YOU!

CONTENTS

1	Introduction	1
2	BTL Mortgages	5
3	Fees	14
4	Tenancy Agreements	19
5	Finding a Property to let out	31
6	Renovating	35
7	Photos from Renovation Projects	53
8	Estimating Costs	72
9	Signing Up on Your Mortgage	76
10	Making an Offer	80
11	Bridging Finance	84
12	Sale Agreed	89
13	Buying at Auction & Auction Finance	106
14	Price Negotiation	112
15	Completion Day	116
16	The Finished House	133
17	Remortgages & Further Advances	137
18	Case Study Introduction	142
19	Case Study 1	144
20	Case Study 2	174
21	Case Study 3	178
22	BTL v. Renovate & BTL	187
23	Flow Charts	191

FOREWORD

I have written this book from the perspective of someone who had little to no real applied knowledge of the property world when first starting out.

What I did have however, was estate agency experience which, gave me the confidence (from years of watching and facilitating the industry) to have a go.

I hope this book gives you a realistic and practical guide into the world of buying and renovating property to let out or sell on. Whether you are a complete novice or even a few houses into your career, it offers a huge amount of practical advice and examples from case studies of my own property purchases, for you to take on board and utilise as you wish. I hope I have given you an honest step by step guide into the property world.

As a small aside: information such as prices, interest rates, stamp duty and rules/laws etc. are subject to change over time and while they are true at the time of writing this book, it is up to you, the reader, to confirm any information is still current before making any decisions.

INTRODUCTION

My name is Christian and I am an entrepreneur. I hate using that term because it makes me sound a little full of myself and also as if I'm a yacht dwelling millionaire, moored off the coast of my tax haven. I can assure you that this couldn't be further from the truth but I'm probably a lot closer to it than the average man on the street. The fact is that in the past (and currently I suppose) I have owned a couple of small on-going concerns (companies if you will) that didn't make me a fortune but kept me in house and home, with a very good work/home life balance. It also gave me plenty of time to dream up and experiment with various avenues of business to pursue.

If nothing else, I am ambitious, creative, organised and manage risk well (in my 'humble' opinion). I stumbled into estate agency in 1997 and apart from a brief couple of years' hiatus as a bank clerk (in many guises), I left the industry in 2004. I had soon come to admire the speculators ('Specs', property developers) rocking up in their fancy cars buying houses as if they were as affordable as groceries and seemingly without a care in the world. They looked self assured masters of the universe and I was in awe of them. It was a lifestyle that looked fairly unobtainable comparing it to my relatively poor (well looked after but skint) upbringing and this lifestyle looked more than appealing. I also had a powerful aversion to being told what to do by people with half my intelligence and working the ridiculously low paid hours estate agency blesses you with.

I'd started my career in estate agency in a period of depression in the market and there were lots of people whose houses weren't worth half of what they'd paid for them in the early 90s. Houses were cheap and mortgages were easy to come by. They were literally giving them away and sometimes they'd even give you 125% LTV (Loan to value) to do the gaff up with; incredible! In 2001 I'd embarked on an Open University degree and whilst still living in comfort with my mum and siblings, was looking to get out of banking (now a tin pot sales job) and work part time to facilitate my way into teaching physics. As luck would have it, my old boss and now friend Dean, gave me a call out of the blue and asked if I wanted to come and work at the Estate Agency he had built up and owned. After some negotiation with regards to the hours, I accepted.

It was 2002 and contrary to every other agent I'd worked for, who frowned severely upon and practically banned you from buying any investment property, Dean was absolutely fine with it as long as you declared your interest to the vendor, so there was no conflict of interest and more importantly, it wasn't a house he was interested in! Everyone seemed to be buying a house to rent out or do up and Dean, who was soon to become my mentor, was absolutely killing it! He still has the agency and 80 houses rented out on his books. In fact, it seemed like the whole of London was buying up houses in South Manchester at the time.

Inspired by this property fever, I purchased my first property with a 100% LTV mortgage. It was a 2 bedroom, 2 reception room house in a quiet little cul de sac, not far from the office. It needed no cosmetic attention and rented out swiftly. Around a year later the market had taken off and prices were starting to rise; accelerating quickly. My tenants were moving out to buy a place of their own and I had the choice of renting again or selling. I enquired as to its value and our manager said it was worth double what I'd paid for it. Happy was an understatement and I couldn't put it on the market quick enough. My colleagues couldn't understand why I didn't want to ride it out and see how high prices went. But I had about £30K equity to bank and I could use that to purchase more houses. I remember thinking I could have invested in 4 with that money but my desire to be self employed and work nearer to home was strong and in a bonkers move I bought a commercial laundry that had been for sale opposite my Mum's house and bowed out of estate agency for the final time, gracefully. My intention had been to save up more money whilst still living at home and reinvesting in the housing market in timely fashion. Unfortunately, for many reasons (mostly tighter mortgage regulations and the clincher; no cash) I wasn't able to rejoin the race until (fortunately) the bottom of another slump in the market in 2012.

Armed with my previous estate agency knowledge, my mentor's example and a 'can do' attitude, I bought my friend's house from him in deepest Stockport as a long term rental investment (like the last one). In almost identical circumstances, a year down the line, the market had performed well and I had about £22K equity in it. I sold the house and used the money to buy an ill-advised (but eventually profitable) renovation project in Tameside and a little, wonderfully decorated, 2 bedroom terraced, with a plush 4 piece bathroom, to rent out, a couple of miles away. In fact I still rent it to this day to the same tenant!

A property developer was born!

BTL (Buy To Let) MORTGAGES

Do you have any savings? This is very important! Cash is king in the property business. Obviously if you are buying solely with cash, but also if you are intending to use a lender to finance your property purchase. Most lenders will lend at 75% LTV (Loan To Value), which means that they will lend you 75% of the property purchase price and you will have to front the other 25%. There are lenders who will lend you 80% of the purchase price but these are few and far between and your interest rates can be substantially higher. There are I believe the odd lenders who will lend 85% but the interest is high and there will likely be high fees and other little pit falls with them too. They seem to be there one minute and then stopped the next, so when budgeting a project I wouldn't hang your hat on the possibility of getting a 15% deposit deal.

Back in the good (not from a world economy perspective, as we've all found out to our cost) old days a 15% deposit was standard and not a decade ago there was a lot more choice of products. But then they became rare and after that so did 80% LTV.

I'm going to assume you have a 25% deposit and any mathematical examples or budgets I present will generally be based on this assumption, as there are plenty of deals available at 75% LTV and currently interest rates are very good as they are based on The Bank of England's base rate. There are also income requirements to adhere to. Most lenders will require you to have an annual income of £25,000-£30,000 before lending to you but there are a handful of lenders that just require you to have an income, as BTL's are self supporting investments. If you are employed then your income is your gross earnings ie before tax is paid. If you are self employed then it is your taxable income, not your turnover. Capital gains does not count and you may struggle to get them to accept rental income too.

You also need to remember that when you purchase a property with a view to letting it out, there are other fees and costs to consider, especially if you are going to renovate a property before you let it out. I will go into these fees at the appropriate juncture but assume if your house purchase is £125K then your fees will range between approximately £7K-£14K depending on your intentions towards the property. This will become clearer as you read further into the book.

Restrictions are also tighter with BTL products, as in the past a lot of people who didn't have the income that met residential criterion for lending, would save up more money and buy a property under the guise of letting it and then just move in. If they couldn't afford the mortgage they would utilise the interest only option and pay about a 1/3 of the monthly price. At the end of the term they would still owe all the capital and if they had no vehicle to repay this, it would land them in big financial do-do. There is the possibility of the property value increasing to cover this but that is a big if! Endowment mortgages also had vaguely similar future reliant issues and they also went the way of the dinosaurs, in hand with self cert., which was a product that lent you 90% LTV and you just had to sign a declaration to confirm you could afford to pay the mortgage! So in 99.9% of cases you need to have a residential mortgage before you can take advantage of a BTL. As a personal example of the restrictions, I was applying to buy a house with my brother, I had a residential mortgage but my brother didn't. They assumed it was a 'back door resi' where we were buying him a house to live in because he didn't fit residential lending criterion. The application was refused.

If you are buying a property solely to renovate and sell on (flip) you should be using cash or bridging finance to fund this type of purchase. A BTL mortgage is intended for you to do just as it says on the tin: buy the house to let it out. This doesn't mean you can't buy it, do it up and then let it out but you are committing mortgage fraud using a BTL to flip. Now this crime is difficult to be caught out at as, if you are smart, there isn't really any policing of this and the real police are generally too tied up with pesky murders and domestic crimes and so forth. However, it is a serious and heavily punishable crime (financial crime usually is) and I am going to assume you are a good boy/girl and are operating legitimately!

What if you don't have the cash to fund a BTL including the fees, nor the money for any necessary renovations? Well there are a few obvious options: You could just sit back and save up more, but it is a fair bit of money to save from scratch. You could borrow the money from a friend or relative (but they are going to need to be confident you know what you are doing). A caveat to this is that under BTL Rules you aren't actually allowed to borrow to invest.

This includes loans, overdrafts and credit cards. If you choose the way people raised money in the 'good' old days through friends/family, they would be required to sign a disclosure form stating that the money is a gift. If you mess up, they have no legal recourse to get the money back; it's a big ask! You could also source an investor to come in on the project with you. You put zero to X amount of pounds in and they fund the rest. It might seem a little unlikely but if you have time and they don't then it could be a marriage made in property heaven. I'm sure there are more options but these are the most likely to my mind. In my own case I started a little business in a sparsely populated sector and saved up money that way. It took time and effort but I'm an assiduous little so and so. For more information and ideas you can purchase my first book: The Apprentice Entrepreneur.

So finally you have the cash (savings). It's OK to browse through the housing portals (Rightmove generally) and do a bit of rough calculating but your next port of call is to make an appointment with a mortgage (and or financial) advisor. Window shopping is all well and good but you need to know that you have the pragmatic ability to purchase. There are mortgage advisors in most estate agents and even though they will charge a fee for the actual arrangement of the mortgage, their advice is free. A little side note: I recommend using a mortgage advisor based at the agent that is marketing the property you are buying. The vendor (owner) of the property you are purchasing is the estate agents client, not you. They are paying handsomely for the service and so their loyalty is to them. It can be argued that keeping the prospective purchaser happy is keeping the vendor happy but essentially you aren't the client and there may be plenty of other purchasers champing at the bit for properties that you are interested in. However, if you are doing a mortgage with them, you also become their client who is paying them a fee and this can raise you up a little in loyalty stakes.

The mortgage advisor will have asked you to bring certain information and documentation with you and during your appointment should usually be able to confirm your viability. On top of that they will hopefully be able to issue you with a certificate to confirm your viability. This is called an Agreement or Mortgage in Principle (AIP / MIP). You can take this to other agents to prove your ability to purchase.

During the appointment, the advisor will likely take you through the choice of lenders, whose lending criterion you fit and go through the different products they can offer you. The main options will be loan to value (LTV) introductory rate: you can choose between a) a variable rate, which will be the highest rate they offer and a certain percentage above the Bank of England base rate, which varies with the economic and political climate. It will cost you more but has the advantage in some cases of having no penalty for leaving the product. This is also the rate that any other product reverts to at the end of its introductory period. b) A tracker rate that is set at a certain percentage above or below the Bank of England base rate. c) The most popular and what, at the moment, I would describe as your 'go to' option in most cases, is the fixed rate mortgage. The fixed rate is a much lower rate than a variable rate to entice you into choosing a particular product. It lasts for a finite period of 2 years, 5 years or even 10 years so you can tailor the product to your individual circumstances. For example, base rate is low and due to the economic or political climate it is likely to increase over the foreseeable future. You may be looking at this rental property as a long term means of income and want to guarantee your income without any anxiety of having to change mortgage products after only 2 years. The interest rates are likely to be higher but that is the price you are paying for longer stability.

There is the method of repayment. You can opt for a repayment mortgage or an interest only product. A repayment mortgage will pay some off the capital of your investment so the amount you owe over time will decrease and you will pay the interest on your loan off at the same time. An interest only mortgage will pay off only the interest you have been charged on your mortgage loan, so at the end of your term you will still owe the amount you initially borrowed. In this case you will need to: complete the sale of the property before your deadline is up, remortgage it if you have the ability, or settle the difference with your own cash. The chances are (based on past evidence) that your property has increased in value significantly (rather than lowered, leaving you in negative equity) and the proceeds from the property's sale will pay off your debt and leave you with a sizeable chunk of money to save, reinvest, blow on a fast car or more sensibly put towards another property or pension.

The duration of the loan. You will be able to take a mortgage loan out for a time period terminating at your government appointed retirement age. So the younger you are, the more time you can take your loan out for, which means you will be paying less back per month.

Fixed rate penalty or penalty associated with another type of product. If you choose to sell the property before your fixed period ends, you are more than likely going to be charged a fee for leaving. In a lot of cases this is usually based on a percentage related to how many years into your fixed fee you have progressed. For example, you are on a 5 year fixed rate: you will pay 5% of the loan amount in the first year of your fixed rate, 4% in the second, 3% in the third, 2% in the 4th and 1% in the 5th.

Arrangement fees. Most products will have some sort of arrangement fee attached to it whereupon, it will be related to the interest rate of that product. For instance you may have chosen a 75% LTV, 2 year fixed rate product, with an interest rate of 2.5% and the arrangement fee is £2995. You may then have the option of the same product where the arrangement fee is £995 but the interest rate has now gone up to 2.65%. Most of these arrangement fees in my experience can be added on to the loan so it will manifest itself in your monthly payments. Your mortgage advisor should be able to tell you if it works out better for you to add it on and pay interest on it or to pay the cash. It will no doubt cost you more money to pay interest on it but how much by will depend on the length of time you own the property for and how much disposable cash you have to start with. Most mortgage products will actually tell you how much you are paying in total so you can compare them.

BTL mortgages currently have a stress test attached to them. Just when you think it's safe to go back in the water! This test is designed to ascertain the combined risk factor of the property, the purchaser and the product. If you go on The Mortgage Works website or just simply Google TMW stress test, you should be able to find a very basic calculator that will tell you what rental income you are required to reach for the product to fit the house purchase. If the property you are purchasing needs renovating, you are inputting the rental valuation in its current state, not the final condition of the property when it is actually rented out.

Are you a 'Portfolio Landlord'? If you are a 'Portfolio Landlord' i.e. you have usually 3 or more properties already let out; beware! Your stress test will be at a higher percentage and so the rental calculation will be less likely to fit i.e. the rental valuation will need to be higher. Some lenders will only allow you to have a certain amount of properties with them before you have to use another lender. Some lenders will only allow you to have a certain number of houses altogether before they will cease to consider your application. Some lenders won't care. But most lenders will want to stress test your entire portfolio and make sure it falls within a certain range eg 75% LTV as a whole. There is some wiggle room in there but not a lot. Also, you will, on occasion, need to prove you have a 'slush fund' ie some back up money in case you are failing to get rent off a difficult tenant or one of your properties is between tenants. I wasn't joking about tighter regulations and using the phrase 'the good old days'.

FEES

I have mentioned fees a lot in this book and I find it handy to have a list in my notes on my phone, so I can do some quick maths when working out the rough viability of a prospective purchase. Below is a list of the fees I use to make my calculations but bare in mind that there will often be some fees such as various admin fees, that get added in here, there and everywhere for anything you try and accomplish.

These fees are based on a purchase price of £125,000 and sale price of £170,000. In this example I am buying the property, taking 6 months to renovate and find a tenant, then selling it whilst still in my fixed period. Hence no remortgage or further advance fees to take into account.

Purchase costs
Financial advisor £500
Mortgage valuation £450
Solicitor for the purchase £1200
Mortgage payments for 6 months £1300
Council tax payments £1000
Stamp duty £3750
Selling costs
Estate agents fee for finding tenant £700
Fixed rate penalty £2500
Solicitor for the sale £1000
Estate agency fee for selling £2000

Total fees £14,400

It's important to remember that some of these costs do not need to be paid until the sale of the property and therefore will not require liquid funds. The last three fees on the list will be taken out of the sale of the property i.e. £5,500. If you are not intending to sell or at least not anytime in the near future, then they can be discounted temporarily or indeed permanently. But if you are intending to sell, then it is important to know that you will incur these costs and they need to be included as outgoings in your profits calculation. On my first renovation project I totally neglected them through lack of experience and the attitude of 'they won't come to that much anyway'. I found out to my cost; they damn well do! On that particular property, had I sold straight away, I would have only made about £5K profit, so I was forced to rent it out in order to maximise the profit that way. I was lucky that I also benefited from a rise in value due to a rising market.

If you have a basic list as shown above, it makes it easier to customise it to your own particular circumstances; it's a good bench mark to have in your head (or on your phone).

It is also important to remember a couple of points:
Estate agency selling fees are usually based around a percentage of the selling price eg 1% with a minimum fee. Estate agency fees for finding a tenant are (in my neck of the woods) a month's rent + VAT.

In recent times there has been a rise in internet based estate agencies e.g Purple Bricks, Strike and Openrent. The latter I highly recommend if you are confident enough to write your own adverts and take the photographs yourself, arrange credit references through them, and do your own accompanied viewings, it is a lot cheaper than a high street agent will charge you. If you have a lot of viewings to organise it can really put a bit of pressure on you but for the financial gain I find it worth the money I save. In recent times I've paid £29 to have my property advertised on all the popular portals including Rightmove and an extra £20 for a credit check on the prospective tenant.

My opinion of the selling agents (not specifically the examples named above) however is somewhat different. In my experience they are definitely cheaper and even free in Strikes' case but when you get to the point of them chasing the sale through, they provide a really subpar service. Although there is a lot of this going on with the high street agents too recently, it doesn't appear to be to the same degree. They just seem to sit back and let all parties carry on at their own pace and rarely know what the current sale status is when you call for an update. If you know the process well then its worth the hassle of doing all the donkey work yourself to save eg £2000 but if not then you may want to stick to a high street agent selling your property for you.

Stamp duty on second properties and the properties after that are taxed on a percentage of the purchase price as follows:

3% up to £125,000
5% up to £250,000
8% over £250,000

Note that stamp duty rates for buy to let purchases are different to those for ordinary house purchases.

Incidentally, when remortgaging, if you are choosing that route, you will be liable as mentioned before for certain fees eg legal fees (although there are products that offer free legal), survey fees (although there are lenders who offer a free survey), FA fees which should be about half their normal rate and the usual admin fees. One of these is a CHAPS payment that you can choose to waiver. It is a same day transfer of any monies you are owed as a result of your remortgage / further advance. If you can wait 3 days for your cash, then they will not charge you for sending it via BACS.

Council tax used to be zero for empty properties for the entire period they were not lived in. Then the exemption decreased to a few months and then weeks. Now there is no exemption. However, if you are doing essential, major repairs in order to make the property habitable, there are exemptions for a limited amount of time.

A final and a very important point: tax is payable on any profit or income you make from property. Income tax on rental income and capital gains tax on any profit from sales. It is VERY important to take advice from a qualified professional with regards to these matters, as they can become rather complicated. For example there are different rules for furnished and unfurnished properties and ordinary lets as opposed to holiday lets. Various expenses can be claimed against rental income, whilst others are claimed as capital expenses. Also note that interest on mortgage type payments can no longer be claimed as an outgoing expense. They are claimed as a tax rebate at 20%, which essentially works out the same but only if you are a basic tax payer; higher rate tax payers lose out using this method.

TENANCY AGREEMENTS

Tenancies are usually between 6 and 12 months in duration and referred to as, 'Short hold assured' tenancies. There are different kinds of rental agreements both residential and commercial but, 'short hold assured' are the ones pertinent to ourselves. In fact when buying with a BTL mortgage, the lender will insist on you renting the property out within a certain time frame (often 30 days) to a professional couple for a minimum lease period of 6 months.

An estate / letting agent will charge you approximately one months rent + VAT to market your property and secure you a tenant. You, of course, are totally within your right to advertise the property yourself. It would certainly be cheaper to make a sign of some description and screw it to the wall or place a notice in the front window for example. However, this does rely on your property having a lot of traffic (footfall or otherwise) passing your property. An agent will not only erect a board, (presumably a more professional looking effort) but will also advertise the vacancy in their office, where prospective tenants are more likely to go to find a rental home, plus they will advertise in newspapers (although this is a little old hat now) and most importantly they will have access to portals like Rightmove where most people will browse for properties for sale and to let alike. You cannot advertise on a portal yourself unless you are registered with them and can prove you are a legitimate estate agency. The agent will also vet the applicants. They will check their credit scores and assess their income to qualify that they can afford the rent. They will attain references to make sure that they have been good tenants in the past. On top of this they may even create an inventory with photographic evidence of the property so that you can compare the condition before and after they were resident. The agent will attend the viewings and move the chosen applicant(s) in when their checks are completed to a satisfactory conclusion. They will also take the tenant's first payment (often a month's rent as deposit plus the first month's rent). They will subtract your fee from that figure and forward you the remainder. Additionally, the agent will produce a tenancy agreement and will obtain the ID and signatures of the applicants. As you can see, going through the agency, although it may look an expensive way of finding a tenant, in the long run, could save you a lot of time and money and make it far less likely that you will end up with a 'nightmare' tenant.

When you have the remainder of the first payment, it will usually be just over the amount that qualifies as their deposit and must legally be placed in a deposit protection scheme such as, 'The Deposit Protection Scheme' - catchy title! They are independent arbiters who hold the deposit funds until the tenant requests them back at the end of their tenancy. They must however have your consent for refunds and if not, then both parties will be required to put their case to the DPS who will arbitrate and divide the funds the way they see fit. This system is to protect tenants from unscrupulous landlords arbitrarily withholding deposits.

Do you want to manage the property yourself? If you use a

letting/managing agent they will deduct from the rental income, which nowadays they insist on receiving and then forwarding to you, a percentage of the monthly income eg 10%. During my career as an estate agent I was charged with many tasks, one of which was to act as a Lettings Co-ordinator for a couple of years. For the management fee, I would check the property once every 3 months to ascertain the condition it was being kept in and supply the landlord with a check list featuring brief descriptions. I would also deal with any complaints from the tenant and organise any repairs and relevant contractors, which the landlord was obliged to pay for. To my mind unless you live far away, this is not money well spent! Hence I manage all my properties myself. It can be a pain at times but generally it isn't 10% of monthly rent's worth of bother.

SAFETY
A few very important things to remember: before you rent a property out to any applicant you must have a gas safety certificate. There are many companies that can provide this service and it costs approximately £70 to have a CORGI registered engineer to come to your property and check that the supply of gas and any appliances are safe to use. You are required to renew this certificate annually. As of April 2021 you are also required to provide an electrical safety certificate. This again is just at the start of the tenancy but only requires renewal after every 5 years. Your only legal responsibility is to ensure that it is safe. On top of this you also need to make sure that you have a smoke detector sensibly fixed to the ceiling of each habitable floor of the property.

INSURANCE

On exchange of contracts of the purchase of your BTL property or in fact any residential property, it is essential that you have building's insurance in place. Your solicitor will remind you and ask for proof. Where this connects specifically with buy to let property is that you will need specific landlord insurance. Go on a compare portal and you will find a multitude of options. As with any property, you can also obtain contents insurance, which might be handy if you are letting the property furnished to any degree but that is up to you to weigh up the pros and cons. The most interesting dynamic of landlord insurance is rent guarantee insurance, which you can tag on to your landlord insurance with a lot of insurers. This, under specific criteria, will cover you for any rent arrears of the tenant.

ASSURANCE

While you are not legally obliged to take out life assurance to pay off your mortgage in the event of your death, you may want to take precautions so that your family doesn't get saddled with the mortgage should the worst happen. The difference between this and the situation regarding your home is that the beneficiary of your will is actually inheriting equity and a business. I would strongly advise you to first of all get a Will written up and speak to your FA regarding life assurances. I am not qualified to advise you further on this subject, I am only offering my opinion.

Reference:

CIA Insurance Services Limited
Houghton Leigh House
Brownsover Road
RUGBY
CV21 1AW

Hazel Grove
Stockport
Cheshire
SK7

7th March 2016

Dear Mr

Thank you for renewing with CIA Insurance Services.

Please read through all of the enclosed documents

As we are authorised and regulated by the Financial Conduct Authority (FCA), we are required to supply you with various documents. In this pack you will find the following documents – **please read them carefully.**

- **How we have met your requirements** – Please check this to ensure that we have understood what you were asking us for. No further action is required if this is correct.
- **Statement of Price** - This confirms the amounts payable by you
- **Proposal Form or Statement of Fact** - If this document needs to be signed, please return this to us.
- **Our Terms of Business with you** – This explains who we are and how we deal with you.
- **A Policy Summary** – This document has been prepared by your insurer to help you to understand your policy. It is important that you read this. In particular the terms, conditions and exclusions. It should be read together with your policy booklet.
- **Your insurance documents including your schedule/ certificate/cover note as required**
- **Your policy document**

Please advise us as soon as possible if any changes need to be made.

Should you have any queries regarding your Insurance, please contact our:
LET PROPERTY CUSTOMER SERVICE TEAM ON 01788 818 600.

To comply with various regulations, in future we will normally only be able to communicate with the policyholder. If you need someone else to contact us on your behalf, please inform us in writing and we will keep a record of your instructions. However, for some transactions, such as renewals, we can only speak to the policyholder.

Yours sincerely

CIA Insurance

Sales: 01788 818 640
Commercial Sales: 01788 818 733
Customer Services: 01788 818 600
Renewals: 01788 818 625
Motor Claims: 01788 818 020
Fax: 01788 818 599
info@cia-insurance.co.uk
www.cia-insurance.co.uk

CIA Insurance Services Limited is an Appointed Representative of Marine Sure, authorised and regulated by the Financial Conduct Authority.
Registered Office: Houghton House, Petitors Road, Rugby, Warwickshire CV21 1AW. Registered in England No. 1933804

23

CIA Insurance Services Limited
Boughton Leigh House
Brownsover Road
RUGBY
CV21 1AW

HOW WE HAVE MET YOUR REQUIREMENTS

This document summarises the details on which your insurance will be arranged.
If any of the information is not correct, please contact us as soon as possible.

We discussed and you agreed that your requirements were:
Let Property Insurance

Endorsements applicable:
As per policy

Property Address:	Croft Street
Building Sum Insured:	£102107.00

IMPORTANT NOTIFICATION
This policy may be based and rated upon the **Buildings Sum Insured (BSI)** which is the rebuild value or reinstatement values of your property as confirmed with us at the inception of this policy.

Please read the following.

As the BSI is a major material fact of the policy we would advise that you check this value is correct to ensure that the cover provided under the policy is adequate as **this may affect any claims which will be paid out on a pro rata basis if the building is deemed to be underinsured.** We must advise that it is the **policyholder's responsibility** to ensure that the BSI is adequate.

If you are unsure or do not know the correct figure, we recommend that you check the Building Cost Information Service website (http://calculator.bcis.co.uk/) to obtain the Rebuild value or refer to a recent survey report which details this figure.

We recommended - TOWERGATE

We have based your statement of demands and needs on the information provided to us

The endorsements relating to your policy are detailed on the enclosed policy schedule

In addition to this, they are also contained in the policy booklet, which will be enclosed with your insurance certificate. If you do require any additional information on these then please contact us. You should carefully read this booklet and take note of the exclusions, excesses, limitations and conditions of the policy.

The policy offered by the above insurer matched the requirements you provided and was charging the lowest premium.

CIA Insurance Services LTD also offer all types of Commercial polices, shop, offices, public houses to name but a few.

Visit our website www.cia-commercial-insurance.co.uk for further information.

Sales: 01788 818 640
Commercial Sales: 01788 818 700
Customer Services: 01788 818 600
Renewals: 01788 818 625
Motor Claims: 01788 818 626
Fax: 01788 818 699
info@cia-insurance.co.uk
www.cia-insurance.co.uk

STATEMENT OF PRICE

CIA Insurance Services Limited
Boughton Leigh House
Brownsover Road
RUGBY
CV21 1HW

Premium for your policy (Including Insurance Premium Tax)	£129.37
Insurer Charge	£0.00
Handling Charge / Discount	£4.58
Total Price	£133.95

The following fees are potentially applicable during the lifetime of this policy

A handling charge of up to £50 will apply to midterm adjustments.
Any refunds following a mid-term adjustment will be paid net of our commission.

If the policy is cancelled within the 14 days cooling off period detailed in the terms of business, then you will only be charged a premium by the insurer representing the time on risk and a handling fee of up to a maximum of £25.
If the policy is cancelled after the 14 days, then a charge will be made by the insurer in accordance with the insurers scale and a refund of premium will be allowed provided that no claims have occurred. We will retain our commission plus a handling fee of up to a maximum of £25

Sales: 01788 818 840
Commercial Sales: 01788 818 733
Customer Services: 01788 818 800
Renewals: 01788 818 825
Motor Claims: 01788 818 830
Fax: 01788 818 699
info@cia-insurance.co.uk
www.cia-insurance.co.uk

CIA Insurance Services Limited is an independent insurance intermediary authorised and regulated by the Financial Conduct Authority.
Registered Office: Newlands House, Ashlawn Road, Rugby, Warwickshire CV22 5QP. Registered in England No. 4332904

ASSURED SHORTHOLD TENANCY

AGREEMENT

For letting a dwelling on an Assured Shorthold Tenancy
under Part 1 of the Housing Act 1988 as amended by the Housing Act 1996.

Important Information for Tenants

This agreement contains the terms and obligations of the tenancy. It sets out the promises made by both landlord and tenant.

Once signed and dated by all parties, this tenancy agreement is a legally binding contract. The tenant is responsible for payment of the rent for the entire term of tenancy. The agreement may not be terminated early unless the tenancy contains a break clause or written permission is obtained from the landlord.

The inventory and schedule of condition should be checked carefully at the commencement of the tenancy. IF YOU FAIL TO AGREE WITH THE INVENTORY AND SCHEDULE OF CONDITION WITHIN SEVEN DAYS OF COMMENCEMENT, IT WILL BE DEEMED TO HAVE BEEN AGREED AND ACCEPTED BY THE TENANT/S. THE LANDLORD MAY THEN RELY ON THIS DOCUMENT AS ACCURATE AT THE END OF THE TENANCY.

If you are unsure of your obligations under this agreement, you are advised to seek independent legal advice before signing.

General Notes

- This tenancy is for the letting, furnished or unfurnished of a residential dwelling. The let will be an Assured short Hold Tenancy within the provisions of the Housing Act 1988 as amended by part three of the Housing Act 1996. As such this is a legally binding document and should not be used without adequate knowledge of Landlord and Tenant law.
- Prospective tenants should have adequate opportunity to read and understand the tenancy agreement before committing to sign.
- This agreement is to be used for tenancies of an initial fixed term less than three years. If the fixed term is for three years or more then the agreement should be drawn up by deed.
- Section 11, Landlord and Tenant Act 1985 – these obligations require the landlord to keep in repair the structure and exterior of the dwelling, and to keep in repair and proper working order the installations for the supply of water, gas and electricity and the installations in the property for space heating and heating water.
- Section 196 of the Law of Property Act 1925 provides that a notice shall be sufficiently served if sent by registered or recorded delivery post (if the letter is undelivered) to the Tenant at the Property or the last known address or left addressed to the Tenant at the property.
- This agreement has been drawn up after consideration of the Office of Fair trading's Guidance on Unfair Terms in the Tenancy Agreement.

of Tenancy Commencement: 31/03/2017

Dwelling Information

Address of Property to be Let: Market Street, Hyde, Cheshire, SK14

Exclusions/Special Conditions. A minimum of one month's written notice must be served to the landlord in order to terminate the tenancy agreement on the 29th September 2017 or thereafter.

Tenancy Information

Initial Term of Tenancy 6 months

Commencement date: 31/03/2017

Expiry date: 29/09/2017

Rental Amount

From	To	Total Rent
Start of tenancy (31/03/2017)	End of Tenancy (29/09/2017)	£475.00 per calendar month

1 Particulars

1.1 Parties

1.1.1 The Landlord(s): Mr

Address: C/O – Fold, Marple Bridge, Stockport, Cheshire, SK6

The "Landlord" shall include the Landlord's successors in title and assigns. This is the person who would be entitled to possession of the Property if the Tenant was not in possession and could be the current Landlord or someone purchasing or inheriting the Property.

1.1.2 The Tenant(s): Mr J & Miss N

Post Tenancy Contact Address: N/A

Contact Tel Number: 07 & 0161

Contact Fax Number: N/A

Contact Email Address: @hotmail.co.uk

The Tenant agrees that Country Holmes may provide the Tenant's name, address and other contact details to third parties including, but not limited to, referencing companies, utility providers, the local authority and the appropriate tenancy deposit protection scheme provider.

1.1.3 Relevant Person

Under the Housing Act 2004 any person or body that provides the tenancy deposit for an assured shorthold tenancy is called a Relevant Person.

The Relevant Person is: The Deposit Protection Service (The DPS)
Contact Address: The Pavilions, Bridgewater Road, Bristol, BS99 6AA
Contact Tel Number: 0844 4727 000
Contact Fax Number: N/A
Contact Email Address: N/A

1.2 The Landlord's Agent

The "Landlord's Agent" shall mean, or such other agents as the Landlord may from time to time appoint.

1.3 The Landlord lets and the Tenant takes the Property for the Term at the Rent payable upon the terms and conditions of this agreement.

To maintain a comprehensive insurance policy with a reputable company to cover the Property, and the Landlord's fixtures, fittings, furniture and effects (including carpets and curtains), but not including the Tenant's belongings.

5.6 That the Landlord will not be responsible for any loss or inconvenience suffered as a result of a failure of supply or service to the Property, supplied by a third party, where such failure is not caused by an act or omission on the part of the Landlord.

5.7 The Landlord agrees to provide a copy of the insurance and any freehold or headlease conditions affecting the behaviour of the Tenant.

5.8 The Landlord agrees to fulfil his repairing obligations contained within Section 11 of the Landlord and Tenant Act 1985. These are quoted below;

11 (a) to keep in repair the structure and exterior of the dwelling-house (including drains, gutters and external pipes);
(b) to keep in repair and proper working order the installations in the dwelling-house for the supply of water, gas and electricity and for sanitation (including basins, sinks, baths and sanitary conveniences, but not other fixtures, fittings and appliances for making use of the supply of water, gas or electricity); and
(c) to keep in repair and proper working order the installations in the dwelling-house for space heating and heating water.

6 The Parties Agree

6.1 Notice is hereby given that possession might be recovered under Ground 1, schedule 2 of the Housing Act 1988 if applicable. That is, that the landlord, used to live in the property, as his/her main home, or intends to occupy the property, as his or her main home.

6.2 The Tenancy may be brought to an end if the mortgagee requires possession on default of the borrower under Ground 2, Schedule 2 of the housing act 1988.

6.3 Before the Landlord can end this Tenancy, he shall serve any notice(s) on the Tenant in accordance with the provisions of the Housing Acts. Such Notice(s) shall be sufficiently served if serve at the last known address of the Tenant in accordance with section 196 of the Law of Property Act 195.

Signature(s) of Landlord(s) or an authorised person of Country Holmes as agent for the Landlord

Signature(s) of Tenant(s)

Invoice

Invoice To:		Job Number:	102
Christian		Invoice Number:	110/46787
Hazel Grove		A/c Ref:	[Optional Ref Code]
Stockport		Date:	11-May-2016
SK7		P/O number:	
		Engineer:	560
		Remedial Authorisation Code :	

Cut your energy bills by installing a new energy efficient boiler. Visit www.gas-elec.co.uk/boilers
Changes to legislation for Carbon Monoxide and Smoke Alarms in rented properties. Visit www.gas-elec.co.uk/alarms

*** Site Address : Market Street, Hyde, Greater Manchester, SK14 ***

Services		Job Reference	Net	Vat @20.00%
G2	Gas Safety Inspection (Report expires 09 May 2017)	CT-110560-	62.00	12.40

Standard certification delivered by the following methods:
Email Delivery to   @hotmail.com for Invoice
Email Delivery to   @hotmail.com for Safety Report

*Payment has already been received in full.

	Totals	62.00	12.40
	Total Including VAT		74.40

In the event of a complaint relating to any service or installation in a property gas-elec must be given the opportunity to address the issue by re-visiting the property to resolve any alleged complaint. gas-elec cannot be held responsible if the opportunity to fully address the matter is not afforded to us. In the event of another company/contractor being called to the property to investigate or attempt to rectify an alleged complaint in preference to gas-elec the company will accept no liability.

Invoiced by:
Gas-Elec Regional Office 110
80 Chapel Lane
Wilmslow
SK9 5JH

Tel: 01625 536 667
Fax: 01625 521 853
Email: area10@gas-elec.co.uk

All payments to:
Gas-Elec Bureau Services
The Old Bakery
14b The Green
West Drayton
Middlesex
UB7 7PJ

Tel: 0844 880 5836
Fax: 01344 572 830
Email: gbs@gas-elec.co.uk

Details for electronic payments:
Natwest Bank
Name: GBS Ltd
Account: 39431460
Sort Code: 60-00-01

Please quote your account number on bacs payments and send a remittance advice to Gas-Elec Bureau Services.

Fenturn Ltd T/A Gas-elec Safety Systems
A company registered in England number 3893227
VAT registration number 738 4018 34

Landlords / Homeowner Gas Safety Record - G2

gas-elec group
The Old Bakery
14b The Green
West Drayton
Middlesex
UB7 7PJ
TEL: 0800 857 8899

Cert. No: CT-11095D-
Site Add.: Market Street
Hyde
Greater Manchester
SK14

Date: Tuesday, 10 May, 2016
Client: Christian
Hazel Grove
Stockport
Cheshire

171224

Gas Installation Details

Meter Reading	Meter / ECV Location	AECV location (if app)	Meter Visual Inspection
CT1	Lounge Cupboard	N/A	Pass

Gas Appliance Details

Location	Kitchen
Make	Revomax
Model #	RSF54ET
Serial #	02617364
Flue Type	Room Sealed
Safety Device	Pass
Operating Pressure/Gas Rate	10.00 mbar
Ventilation Adequate	Yes
Flue Flow Test	N/A
Spillage Test	N/A
Termination Satisfactory	Yes
Visual Condition	Pass
Appliance Serviced	No
ID, AR or Advisory situation	Advisory Notation
Gas Council Number	Not Found
Flue Gas Analysis (Ratio)	0.0038
Safe To Use	Yes
Appliance related comments	MHG pipes to not turned downstream on the outside wall

Meter Type	ECV Accessible	Gas Installation Pipework	Let By/Tightness Test	Record Pressure Drop	Protective Earth Bond
BB	Yes	Pass	Pass, Pass	0	Yes

In the event of a complaint relating to any service or installation in a property you visit, must be given the opportunity to address the issue by re-visiting the property to resolve any alleged complaint (gas-elec cannot be held responsible if the opportunity to fully address the matter is not allowed us). In the event of another company/particular being called in the property to investigate or attempt to rectify an alleged complaint in preference to gas-elec the company will accept no liability. A detailed internal inspection of the flue integrity, construction and timing has not been carried out. I confirm that the satisfactory records above has been examined and brought to the attention of the Responsible Person in accordance with the GSIUR and Gas Industry Unsafe Situations Procedure This report has been completed and issued by gas-elec safety systems Ltd part of the gas-elec group.

Next Inspection Due Within 12 Months

This Safety Record Issued By

Name

Page 1 of 1

FINDING A PROPERTY TO LET OUT

First of all you need to confirm the strength of the letting market in the areas you are searching within. It is also advisable to check surrounding areas to assert the ratios of property prices compared to rental prices. For instance adjacent areas may have similarly priced properties but one may have a rental valuation that is a little higher and all things being equal you would choose that area.

What level of furnishing are you looking for? You will understandably receive a higher rent for a nicer decorated property. You will also likely be able to rent it out for more monthly income too. In tandem though, you will also have to pay more for a higher spec house, so it's swings and roundabouts. Your affordability could well dictate the choice for you.

Are you going to rent the property unfurnished, furnished or part furnished? When you furnish a property you can ask more money for the rent; that is the upside. You are also then responsible for maintaining and or replacing the items included in your contract and also it can actually put people off renting your property because most people, certainly serial renters will have their own furniture. On the other hand, you may want to consider what kind of tenant hasn't even got any furniture? That comment may sound harsh and isn't entirely accurate. There are many reasons someone may have no furniture: victims of crime, especially domestic crime, people new to the country and people who are young and looking to move out of home for the first time and probably more.

Many mortgage companies used to specify that your tenants must be professional, working occupants so as to ensure the likelihood of you being paid your rent every month and on time. This was deemed to be discriminatory in law and they are now not allowed to stipulate to this. I have been in a position where I have been in receipt of benefits such as: income support, housing benefit and working tax credit and I wouldn't consider myself an unreliable payer, in fact I have a perfect credit score on Experian. But I suspect it is no coincidence that the only houses I rent out where there are difficulties with either the rent being paid on time or the condition the property is being kept in, are the only properties with benefit receiving occupants. Maybe coincidence?

Will you need to renovate the property fully or just in part? If there is any equity to be made from a house that needs work and there is a resulting uplift in value then, if you have the time and the cash to do the work, this is often the most savvy way to operate. This could be a property with say a £30K potential price increase which would not only be worth renovating and flipping but would also give you the option to buy the house, do it up, rent it out and remortgage in 6 months time in order to liquify some of your asset, freeing it up for future investment. Your small profit will be partially in the money you receive as change from paying your previous product off and the rest will sit as equity in the property. If these last few sentences aren't making any sense, don't worry, I will be including a much clearer explanation later on in the guide as part of a case study, to show you in stages how this process works.

To compare the profitability of your potential acquisitions, you can calculate the rental yield using a simple calculation:

Annual Rental Income / Property Value X 100 = Property Yield

A great yield is 8% or more but I have plenty that are at 4% and I'm doing ok.

Your next step is to actually start browsing the property market. You can go into estate agents and ask to be registered on their mailing list but they won't really have one that is tailored exactly to your market and if it is a renovation project you are looking for, then join the queue. If you are new to the game, then you will be at the back of the list. The specs with experience and more importantly past form with that agent, in fact more accurately, that particular office, are the ones (if any) who will get a call. Your best bet is to keep your eyes glued to Rightmove or other portals to get the best chance of finding something suitable. You can set up alerts that will buzz you as soon as a new property comes on the market. But this can get very annoying as very few of them will be of interest and you will get alerted a lot. You can also source different auction companies and browse their sites and catalogues for bargains but as you learned earlier, auction purchases can be difficult (at least at first) to navigate and you may have to depart from BTL finance.

Once you have found a property of interest then you need

to arrange a viewing; the sooner the better! If it is a bargain, you can expect to be amongst a great many prospective buyers wanting to view. In fact, if a property is very popular, you may be booked into a block viewing where many viewers view at once. You will certainly find this happening with auction properties. If you are keen on the house and the figures stack up, then it is time to think about an offer. I will come back to this in a few chapters as there are other points to cover first.

RENOVATING

Choosing a property to renovate is one thing: doing the actual renovating is a much taller ask - much taller! But this doesn't mean it is impossible; in fact far from it. Thousands of people across the UK are doing exactly that and I am one of them. I learnt through trial and error as well as taking some excellent advice from a contractor (who was quite the double edged sword when it came to convenience but a wealth of excellent tutelage!). Here I will impart the way I now approach any renovation project. It isn't fool-proof but anyone who has a 'foolproof' way of doing anything is most likely a snake oil salesman.

Most speculators will look for property at the cheaper end of the market so as not to exhaust precious liquid funds (cash). Don't get me wrong, there are much, much bigger profits to be made in larger projects: building new homes, knocking down mansions and building even bigger mansions in their place and converting office / light industrial space into apartments etc, but they all require huge cash reserves in the coffers. I'm assuming that you are not there yet. Also it's important to remember that the more affluent an area you purchase your property in, the higher the standard and the more cash you'll require to elevate its standard to. On top of this can you imagine (or work out in 20 seconds with a calculator) what the stamp duty would be on a 6 bedroomed detached home in Wilmslow.

On a slight tangent, briefly, if you are straying into the commercial / industrial property world you will do well to remember a couple of things. First of all you must remember that there is not only a monthly payment for your finance to pay while you are renovating the property, there are also business rates to pay (akin to council tax) and these can be sky high. They really can be the make or break of a project. If you want to convert a commercial or residential property into separate apartments, you will most likely need planning permission even when the .gov site tells you otherwise. If the property has a mortgage of any description on it, you need to confirm with the lender that they are okay with you splitting the title or consolidating the title in the reverse case; because they generally aren't. In lots of cases you need to: buy cash or bridge, have planning permission and then legally split the titles before eg. remortgaging them or selling them to exit the project. Now I am no expert here and I would advise you to take professional advice if you intend to travel this road or are sat at an auction and see something too good to be true. Auction fever can make you extremely rash!

A very experienced property renovation company director (Walt, a legend in west Manchester), I employed back in my less experienced days and still do now on occasion advised that you should look to make about 15% gross profit on a renovation. But even if you fall short, 'it's better to earn 10% of something than 15% of f*#k all'. By this he meant that you may as well keep investing your money rather than waiting for the ideal project to come along. He also said that whatever project your investing in, it's better than leaving your money in the bank at today's interest rates. A caveat to this is that while you have invested all your capital into a less than large profit yielding project, you may then miss a project that was much more preferable. Although one in the hand is worth two in the bush. Ya pays ya money, ya takes ya choice and several more tired old cliches.

Let's do a little maths:
If you were to purchase a property for £125K and spend £14K on fees and then £20K on renovation then multiply to find out what 15% of that was: £(125+14+20)K X 1.15 = £182.850. This final figure is approximately what you hope the final valuation of your renovation project will be valued at. So if you minus your expenditure from that figure, it will give you your estimated profit (before tax): £182,850 - £159,000 = £23,850.

Back in the day when I was first an estate agent, specs were treated like royalty. It appeared to everyone that they were doing you (the agent and the vendors) a favour by purchasing their dilapidated homes and repossessed properties (and there were a lot back in those days). It seemed like they were doing everyone a solid by mopping up all the unwanted houses that nobody could afford to, or wanted to restore, to a habitable living space; maybe they were? The manager of the branch would have his or her favourites and call them up as soon as something came on the market. They were the investors who were reliable, efficient and usually had the funds to do multiple projects, ie. a proven track record. They would be handed these little gold mines on a silver platter and keep you all sweet with little gifts at Christmas from their exotic travels. These weren't kick backs (that would be unethical and cost them a lot more money). I'm sure there must have been agents out there taking bungs but none that I ever saw. I may sound a little jealous . . . Cos I am! But good on them, they saw an opening, had the balls to risk their capital and they are mostly probably stinking rich by now (at least the ones I know are).

In the late 90s the market was on its arse and many people were in negative equity with their mortgage lenders i.e. If they sold their home there wouldn't be enough money to settle their debt. These people were stuck in properties and unable to move. Therefore the bottom of the market had stalled and this had a knock on effect. Lending rates were high and unemployment had been high, so lots of people had no money to buy and lots of people hadn't got the ability to sell; what a pickle! There was some respite in the guise of 'Let to Buy' mortgages which allowed you to let your own house out in order to get finance on your ongoing purchase.

As I mentioned at the introduction, in the early 2000s they were giving mortgages away like sweeties and this really got the market moving. Obviously there was a 'small' price to pay later that decade and we are still paying for it now to some degree. This is where I first cut my teeth in the property business.

Choosing your project. If you have a little form you may still have estate agents who will give you the nod about a good deal on the horizon but generally you are firmly in the arena of checking Rightmove every other day or so to see if anything takes your fancy. I will usually put my own postcode in the relevant box and then set a search area radius that I'm prepared to stretch to and a price that I can afford at the time. Maybe a little higher in case I can negotiate that particular vendor down enough. You may be left with quite a lot of houses to read through but my brother noticed that there are often very few photos on the houses that need work (should have been obvious really) so you can scan through looking for the number of photos posted in the corner rather than clicking on and searching through the interior photos. It's not fool-proof but it's a good time saver. You can also set a property alert so you will be contacted when a new property comes on the market fitting your criterion but if you have cast your net wide this could get very irritating, as there are no boxes to tick that specify renovation project.

So let's set up an ideal scenario: you find a property within a few miles of where you live. This is ideal so that in the future it is convenient and expedient to commute to the property to work on it yourself or check on the progress of the contractors you have employed to help renovate the property. You've analysed your comparable sales in and around your street and found a property 10 doors down with the same footprint as yours. That sold for £50K more than the one you are looking at and it was in good decorative order, plus it completed only half a year ago. You can ask estate agents for this information or check Zoopla and Rightmove, 'nearby sold prices'. It is important to check the dates your comparables were sold at as it will give you a much better idea of how much credence you can give to this evidence. If it's 2021 now then a property's completion price from 2004 isn't going to be much help. There are other aspects that you need to check on. Photographs will help you suss out if the property was in a decorative state akin to your planned spec. The selling agent may give you some useful information as well as their opinion on the future valuation of your, to be, renovated property. You can enquire as to how long the property took to sell and how popular the street / area is.

Side note: if you purchase a property from a certain estate agent and complete in a timely manner, they will recommend you to the next vendor whose house you may purchase through their branch. This goes double if, when you have completed the work you then sell or let the property out back through them. It is generally considered good form to do so and will work in your favour in the long run.

Building relationships with estate agents (actually with anyone throughout your life I suppose) is hugely beneficial and can save / make you money. A vendor would be silly to take an offer a few percent higher than you are offering, from an unknown quantity than from a tried and tested performer such as yourself. Also if you are buying (certainly with cash) but sometimes with a BTL mortgage it is likely you are paying a much higher deposit and when the survey comes back, the lender will be far less picky with the results. There are two reasons for this: one, you are less of a risk as they are lending you less money and two, you are seen as less of a risk, because you are considered as knowing what you are doing as compared to e.g. a FTB (First Time Buyer) struggling to get on the ladder on a 95% LTV product.

Now for instance this house you have your eye on is on the market for £125,000 and your comparable sold in about a month, 6 months ago. It's décor wasn't top spec but not a million miles away. You confirmed your buying capability with your FA and your MIP is nestled comfortably in your back pocket. It's time to view!

Obviously you are keen to get in there, make an offer and get SSTC (Sold Subject To Contract) on the sale board (or just Sold) as soon as possible, on the viewing you do not want to quickly scan the interior of the house and miss some problem that can impact on the future success of this project such as, the giant crack in the outrigger or that enormous bulge in the side elevation. It is ideal to be able to take a surveyor (which will cost) or an experienced builder to come and give it the once over, but it's not always possible to get someone on short notice and you might just have to suss out any problems yourself. As you progress deeper into your renovation career you will gain much experience and it will become second nature to spot (even just the warning signs) of any potential problems. There is no need to panic too much about structural movement, as the lender will insist on sending in a surveyor and he should route out any glaring defects that could prove risky to them and you.

Side note: mortgage companies will send out a valuer to check the property is worth what you / they are paying for it. If a surveyor / valuer identifies any potential warning signs, they will insist on you commissioning a builder, electrician etc or even a structural engineer to ascertain any pertinent issues. So if something does come to light and there is going to be some hefty costs involved, you can bow out if you wish and only be a few hundred quid down, as opposed to thousands. That's not to say that structural issues aren't surmountable but if you are a novice it might be just as well to leave them to the pro's, unless they aren't too complicated e.g. missing lintels, minor bulges in brick work and so on. After the structural report is submitted then the lender will ask you to arrange a builder to go into the house and quote for that work to be done and on receipt of that report, will offer its criterion for you to continue with the application; or not in some cases. This is why it can be just as good and free to get an experienced builder to go with you; they can be very knowledgable. If you hand him/her some or a lot of work, in return it will have been worth the effort for them and another relationship has been built (hopefully with no structural problems).

If you are going to venture in alone; fear not. I have many tips for you to look out for when you embark on your tour of the property:- First of all get there early. You can sometimes feel pressured by the person showing you around to be swift. If you beat them to the viewing, you can relax and take in the exterior of the property in your own time. True, you can always do this after but you may forget and have to come back. Also bring a note pad and paper or tablet if you're not a middle-aged Luddite like me and a camera (obviously integrated into your tablet or phone). This way you can refer back to the information at a later date with clarity and you may also see something on a picture that you missed first time around.

Following is a list of general things to look for. It is by no means exhaustive but it has stood me in good stead for analysing the condition of a property. You will need to have a good idea of the work involved, as you are likely going to want to make your first offer when you've got back home.

ROOF

Bowing in the roof (dips):
May have been failure in one or more rafters or purlins.

Missing or dislodged tiles:
Creates leaks.

Chimney straight:
If the chimney is not structurally sound it may need rebuilding or taking down altogether. Removing a chimney all the way down to the ground floor is a fairly big job but you can always support missing sections with a lintel.

Pointing adequate:
A lack of mortar between bricks and tiles can invite penetrating damp and leaks.

Flashing in place:
Another opportunity for water to get in to the property.

Gutters performing their duty correctly:
If the gutters aren't directing water away correctly or not

catching it at all, then you can invite leaks and damp into and around the property.

EXTERNAL WALLS

Cracks, especially wide cracks:
Often cracks are benign and a result of settlement over time. But in some cases they can be very serious indeed and point to ongoing structural problems. This is probably one of the largest concerns. Check that the cracks aren't mirrored on the internal walls, which can be indicative of this sort of issue. On the other hand the cracks I usually see are above and below windows which are often a sign of missing or defective lintels; not a major issue on the whole. Also bulges in brickwork can signal that the outer skin of the wall is moving away from the inner and needs tying or rebuilding.

WINDOWS

Double glazing:
Are the windows PVCu double glazed? Most buyers will want to see double glazed windows in a property because: they are far less maintenance than timber, look nicer than steel and are more energy efficient. Replacing a full set is a large outlay. Also check the units haven't cracked, this can point to a structural defect, usually lintels. Trapped condensation will suggest that the inside unit needs replacing. Also check timber frames aren't rotten. You may have some beautiful, antique, sash windows you'd do well to hang on to.

INTERNAL WALLS

Cracks again:
Check that internal cracks don't match external ones. A lot of the time inside the property, cracks will be a result of settlement but can be due to poor decorating or heat expansion of joinery or plaster - or those pesky lintels again.

Damp:
Rising damp will manifest itself up to approximately 1m in height up the wall, any higher than that you can assume that it will be caused by leaks or condensation. Sometimes leaks can be caused by failed plumbing and condensation can simply be due to a house being left empty with no heating. Penetrating damp may be down to ineffective pointing externally. Rising damp however is a result of atmospheric pressure pushing ground moisture through the capillaries in the walls and will be caused by a failure or a lack off a damp prevention system. A full DPC (Damp Proof Course) on a large house can come to a fairly large figure but comparatively inexpensive in the grand scheme of things. It is something that you should almost expect to have to budget for as it is a more common occurrence than one would imagine. A damp contractor will come and quote for this, for free in most cases. You can purchase a damp meter for very little money and check the walls yourself while viewing.

Plaster:
In the majority of cases you will need to re-skim the plastering on the walls to attain a presentable finish; an

additional repair you should assume in your costings. If there are large chunks of plaster missing then the wall may require more than some dot 'n' dab, it may need partial or full plastering which will add significantly to the cost.

FLOORS

If the floor is made from concrete you need to check for damp. If it is damp then it will likely need to come up and be replaced and have a damp proof membrane installed.
Usually floors are made from wood, a combination of floor boards fastened to load bearing joists spanning each room. These can also be damp and/or rotten. Damp can often spread from the walls and it was common place for mortgage valuations to ask for a Timber and Damp specialist to provide a further report and a quote. On a residential property this is probably still common but with a BTL Mortgage you are likely to be left to your own devices and it may not even be mentioned. There are other afflictions that the wood work can be affected by including dry rot and wood worm. I'm not sure if this technique is akin to kicking the tyres while viewing a car but jumping up and down at the corners of a room can provide evidence by way of springiness as you land. Careful though, I went through a (luckily downstairs) floor doing this; it certainly clarified the floors integrity. Joists and floor boards can be replaced though.

CEILINGS

Cracks are common in ground floor ceilings because of reverberation from upstairs and from general heat expansion. Most of the time they will just need a re-skim. Any discoloured patches may indicate a leak eg from faulty plumbing. Upstairs is almost the same procedure but any leaks are more likely to be from roof defects as mentioned earlier.

LOFT

Another chance to check out the roof but from the inside. An overhaul can be relatively cheap but if a whole new roof is required, that can be very costly. Examine the space in this area also. It could be worth converting into a new bedroom. This may require planning permission depending on how 'converted' it already is. You may get away with just the building regulations but you will need to install natural light, a fixed stairway with its own access and much larger joists. The joists originally installed in the loft space are not load bearing so you can't put anything too heavy up there safely. The cost and time taken to convert can often outweigh the benefit from the increase in value that an extra bedroom will provide.

CELLARS

Cellars can be a little gem and an excellent blank canvas for a new useable room. You need to assess how high they are and if they are worth converting or will just have to suffice as a storage area. Your big issue here is our old pal damp. Cellars are usually below any damp course installation and it is pot luck as to how dry they are. You can 'tank' it. Tanking is expensive and so it is unlikely to be worth the cost in pursuit of achieving a much higher rent and/or valuation on the property.

HEATING AND PLUMBING

Is there a gas connection? It's not the end of the world if there isn't because it isn't that expensive to have Cadent come and connect it from the road. Be aware though that this may vary according to location. If you are far away from the main pipe and you are building new homes for example, then it's a different ball game.

Investigate the age and condition of the boiler. In my experience boilers are the biggest cost with regards to repairs and/or replacements during a tenancy.

A full gas central heating system is a real bonus because it needs to have one realistically if you want to elevate the property to its full potential and attain the most equity and rent. If the piping is there and the boiler is in fair condition, then replacing radiators isn't too expensive, apart from a fancy one in the bathroom and kitchen.

Make sure there is no lead piping as it will need replacing and the central heating pipes are the correct width. Also make sure there are taps and drainage in the usual places.

ELECTRICS

In the majority of cases a full or a part rewire will be necessary. Check the age of the consumer unit and the location and age of the sockets and light switches. You can no longer have sockets fixed in skirting boards or bare wiring.

DÉCOR

What can you salvage? Original features: nice cornices, ceiling roses, sconces, solid doors, cast iron fire surrounds, useable architraves, wood burners, ranges etc, etc; the list of examples is long. A mix of original features in a modern surround is a very saleable / rentable design.

GARDEN / PLOT

Most of the time this is a job that requires a bit of your own elbow grease. In some cases, with larger properties, the cost of landscaping can run into tens of thousands of pounds and can break a project; though unlikely in a 2 bed terraced.

Check the boundaries are clearly defined. Legalities regarding land borders can drag on indefinitely.

Are the gardens enclosed or shared access?

Most importantly it is more than ideal to be gifted with off road parking especially in cities and other built up areas where parking is at a premium. To qualify the kerb must have been dropped to allow access over the pavement to your property.

With regards to renovating you can expect to pay as little as £10,000 (less if you are lucky) or as much as, well the sky's the limit. I would say though on a 2 or 3 bedroom terraced or semi detached property you shouldn't be paying any more than £30,000 - £35,000 even with VAT. Believe me there are plenty of contractors who are more than capable and not VAT registered. You will find it more difficult with a contractor who can do the full renovation 'in house'. If you are not VAT registered yourself this can be a huge expense; one to be avoided if possible.

When instructing a contractor it is important to get a fixed price rather than someone charging you a daily rate and potentially working at their own pace. Also you will want to discuss a pay structure eg half up front and half after the work is completed; a proportion of the fixed completed works cost or maybe you pay for materials and pay for the Labour at the end of the job.

You can save yourself a lot of liquid funds by using a big commercial store like B&Q. They do a range of finance coupled with trade discount and in some cases they will facilitate 12 months interest free credit, buy now, pay in 12 months. If your project is going to cost £15,000 you have just saved yourself from laying out £5K. That could be used toward a new venture or many other outlays, certainly if you are renovating multiple properties.

When works have been done you will need the relevant paperwork to prove the renovation has been completed to a legal standard.

CERTIFICATION

FENSA certificate for new windows
Electric work should be signed off by an electrician with up to date NICEIC qualifications
Gas work should be signed off by a CORGI registered engineer
Planning certificates should be obtained for any necessary building work or alterations

Building regulations should also be obtained as they are legally necessitated
DPC guarantees should be retained
Gas safety certificates obtained prior to letting out the property
EPC (Energy Performance Certificate)

OTHER SAFETY STANDARDS

It is your responsibility to ensure that the electrics and gas are safe. You can usually get safety certificates from the same company you procured your gas safety certificate from. This is now mandatory!

A smoke alarm on each floor used for living accommodation.

Carbon monoxide alarm anywhere near where you are burning solid fuel (eg wood, coal) or gas.

Free from potential hazards such as: full glass internal doors, lead piping and asbestos.

Check that there is: adequate heating, a good water supply, sufficient lighting and decent security.

Also check that there are none of the following: damp and mould (as these are health hazards), trip and fall hazards, fire risks, electrical hazards, overcrowding, excessive noise, pests and vermin; chemicals and hazardous substances or structural defects. For more explicit descriptions of these terms see www.gov.uk

THE FOLLOWING PAGES CONTAIN A SELECTION OF BEFORE & AFTER PHOTOS TAKEN IN SOME OF THE PROPERTIES THAT I HAVE RENOVATED.

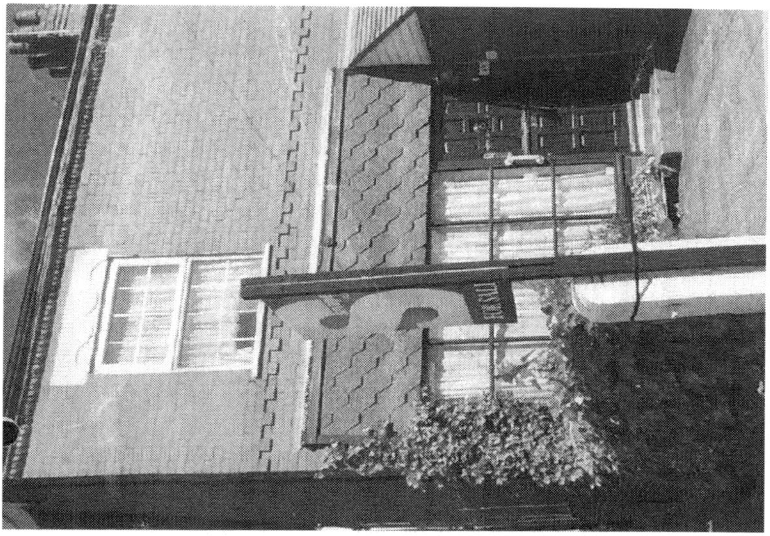

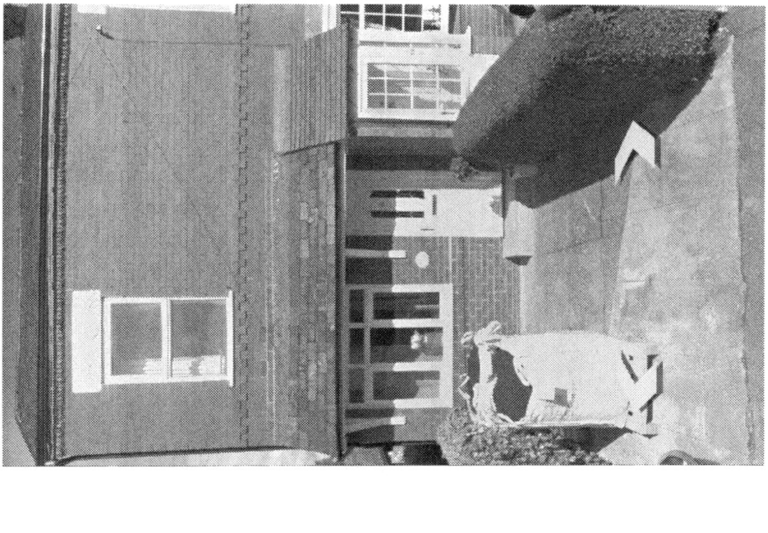

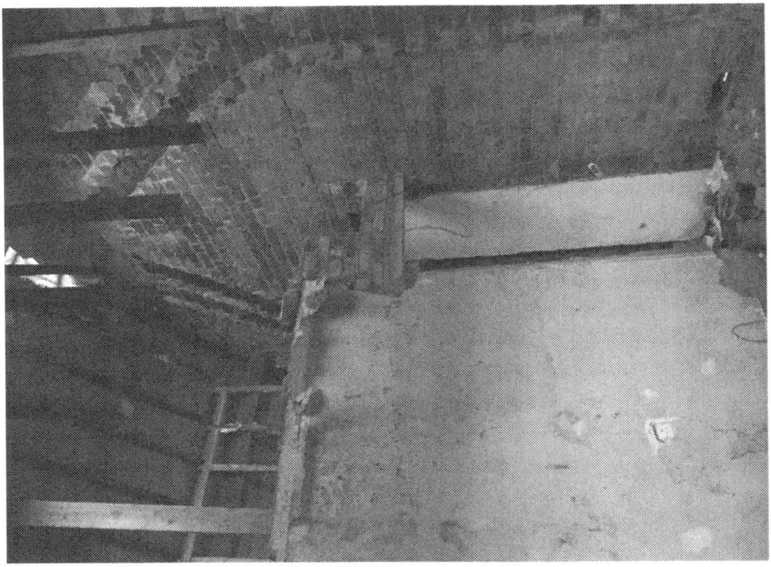

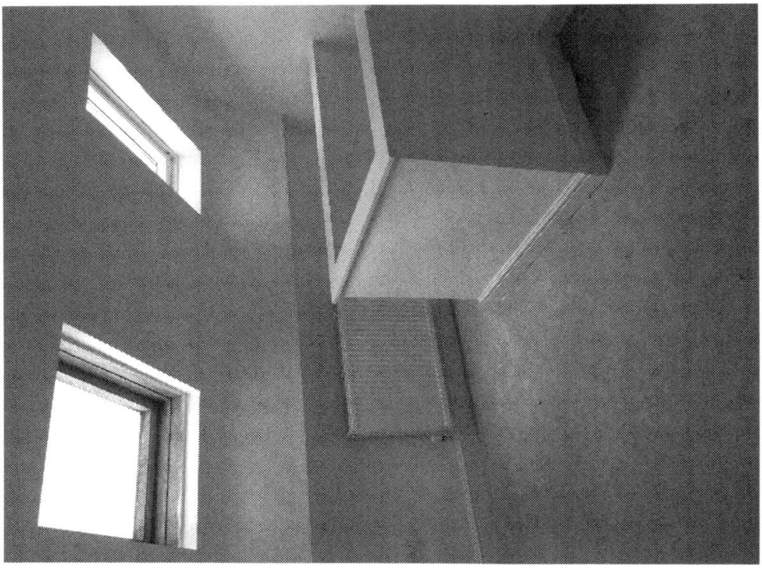

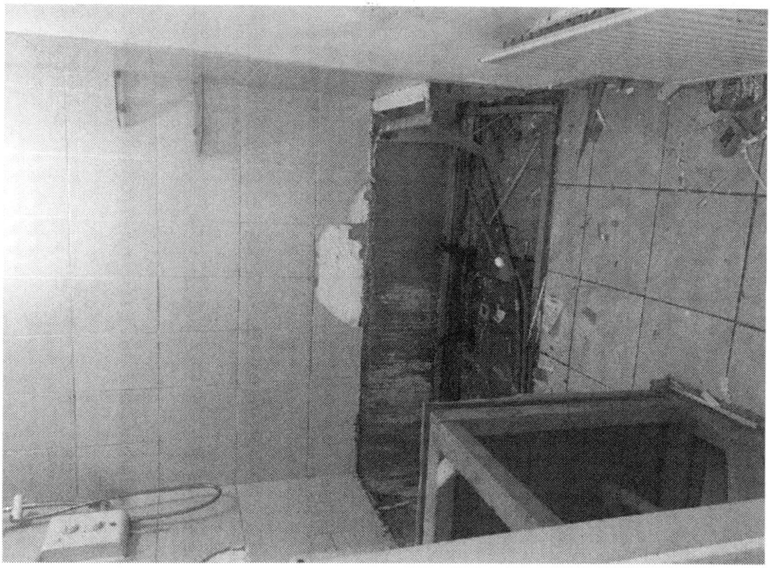

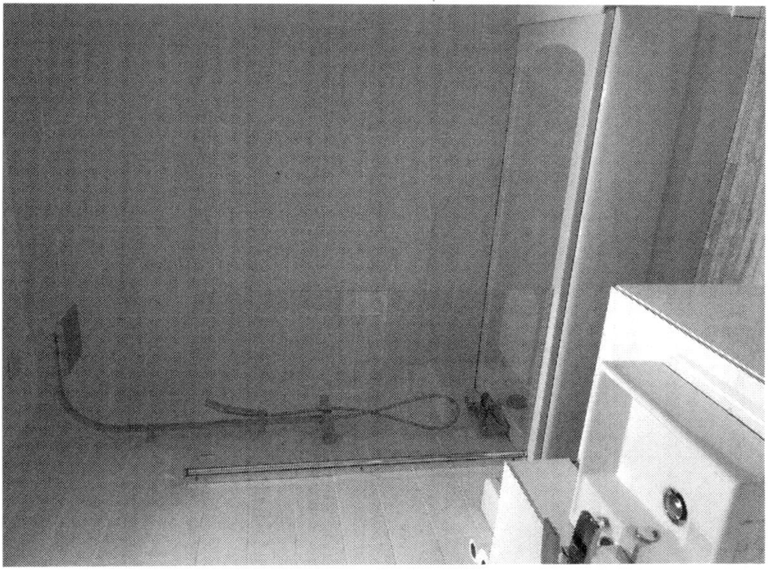

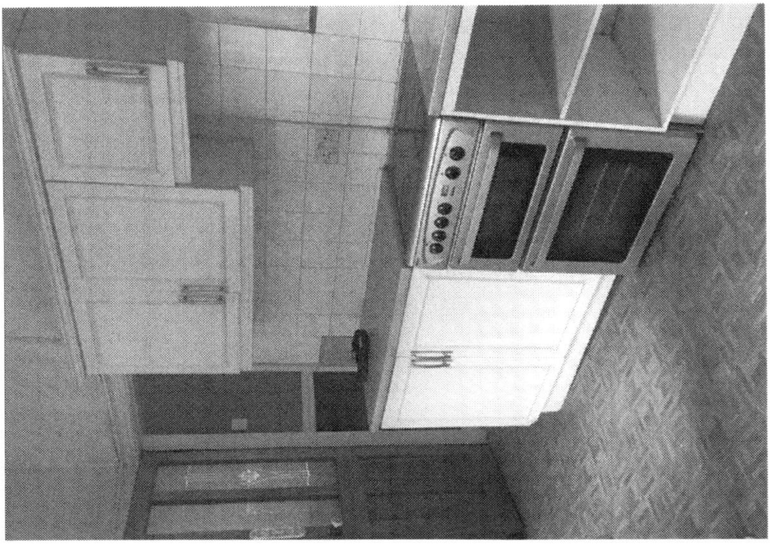

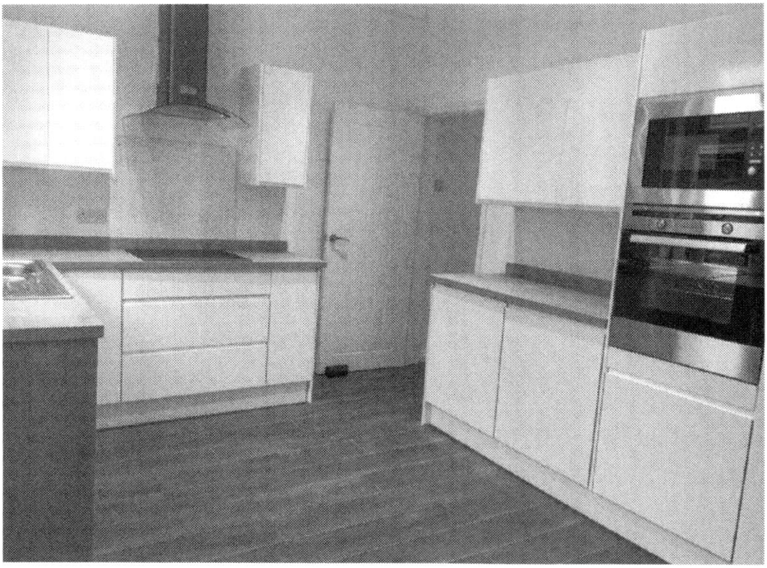

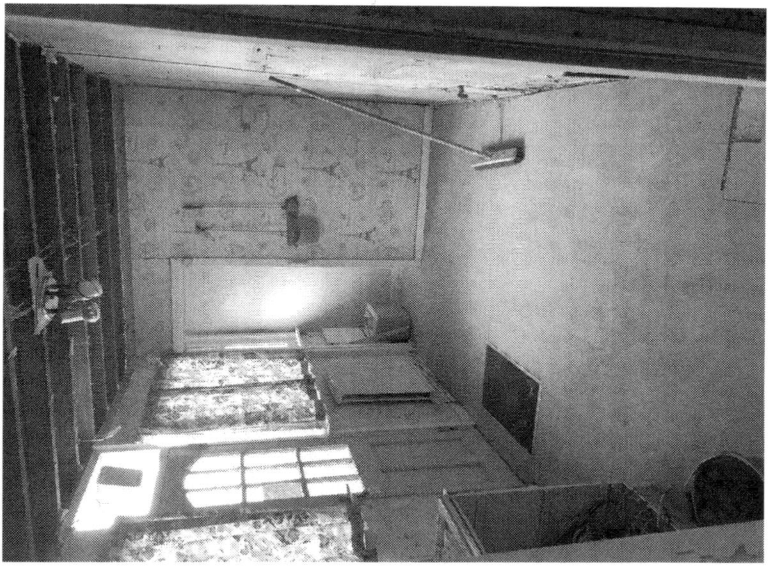

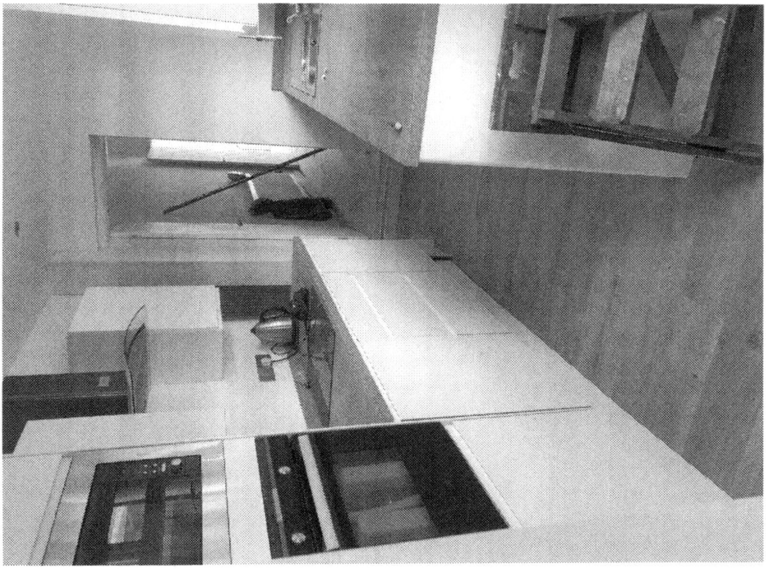

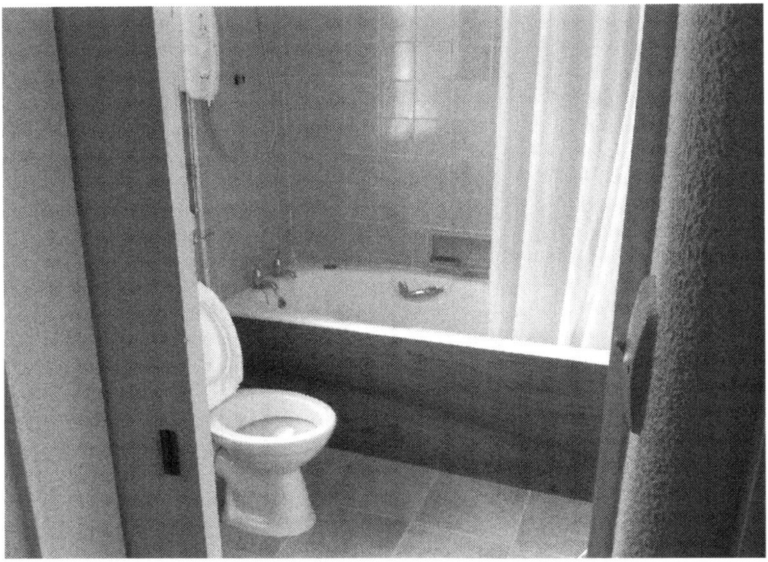

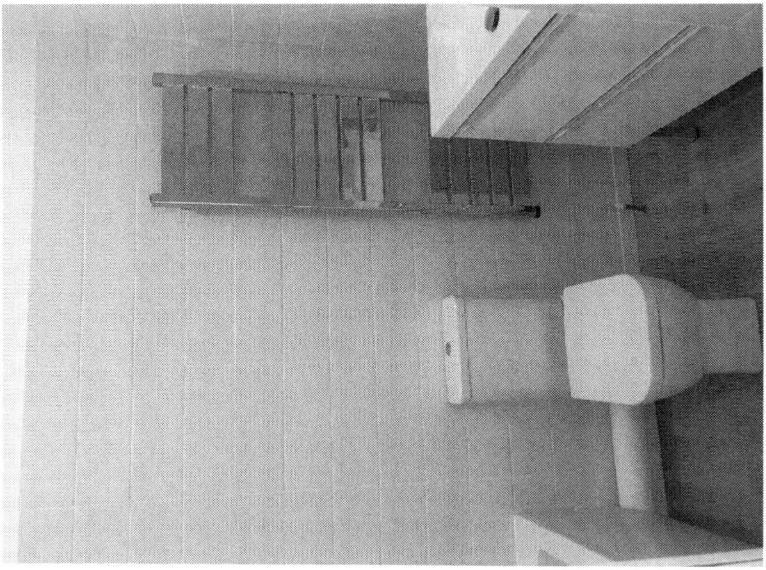

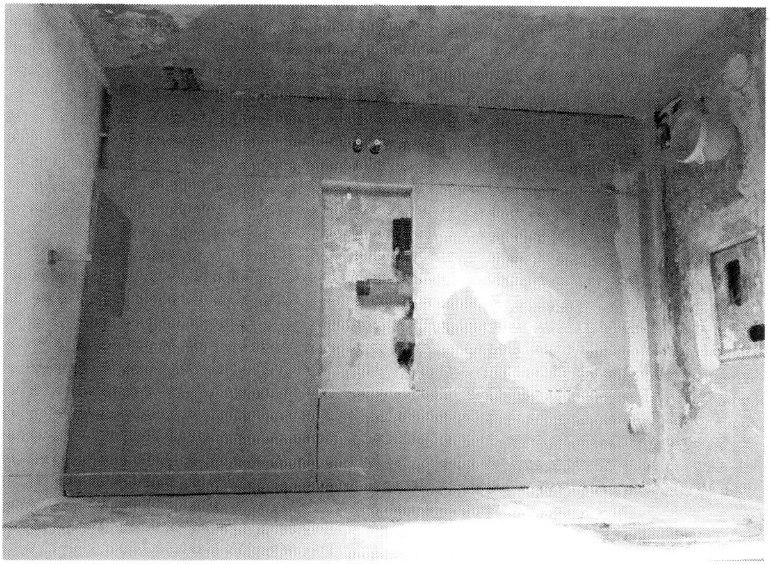

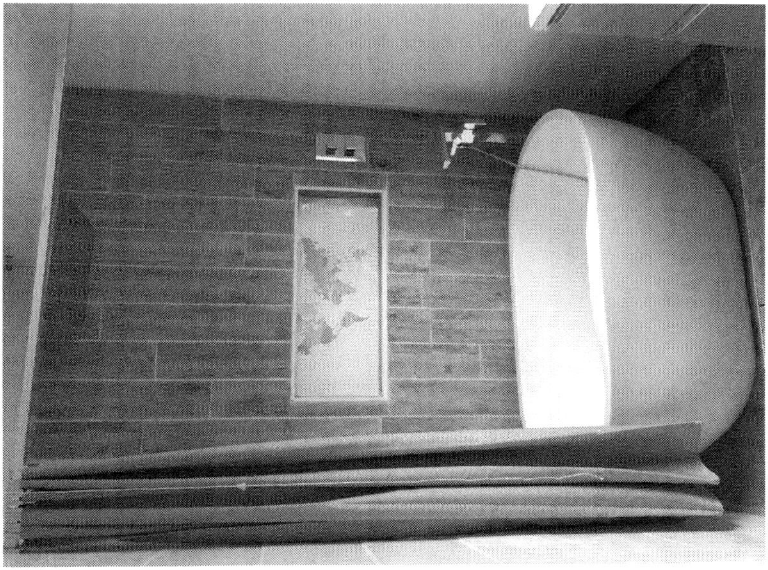

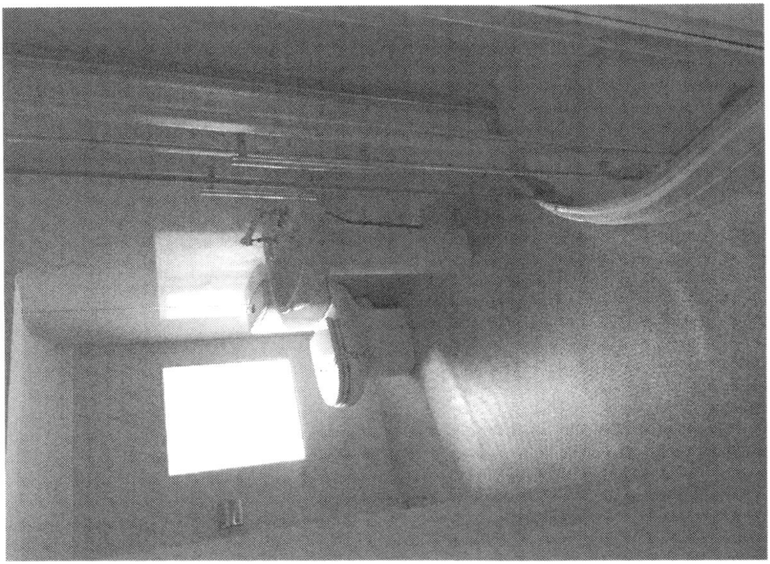

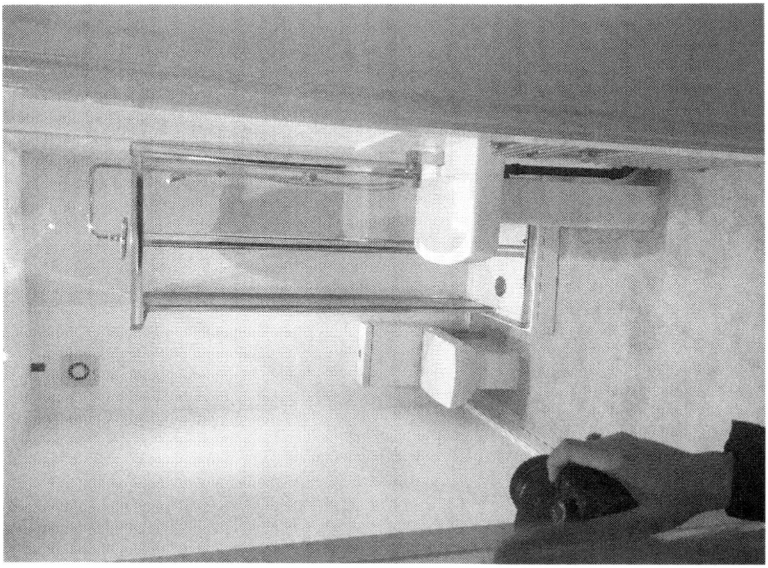

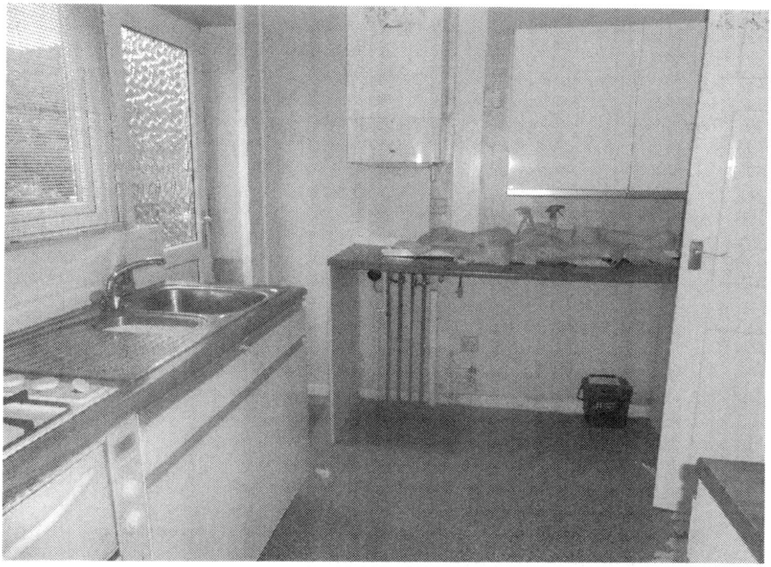

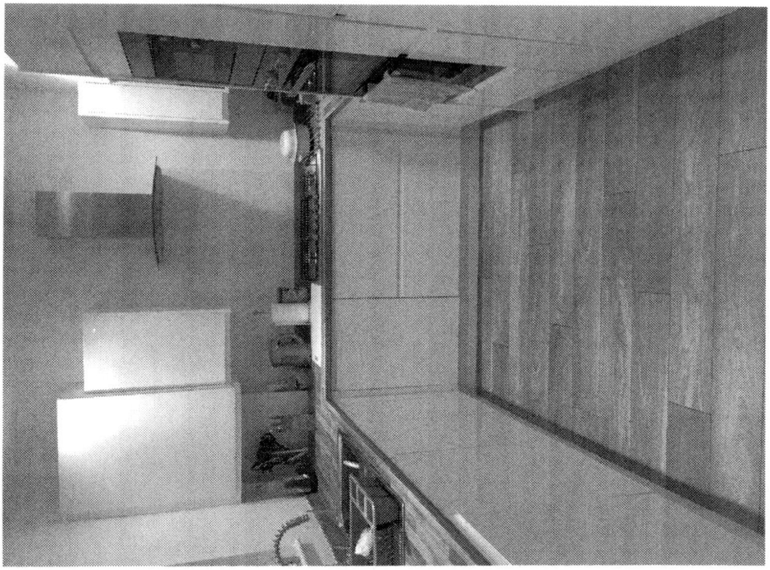

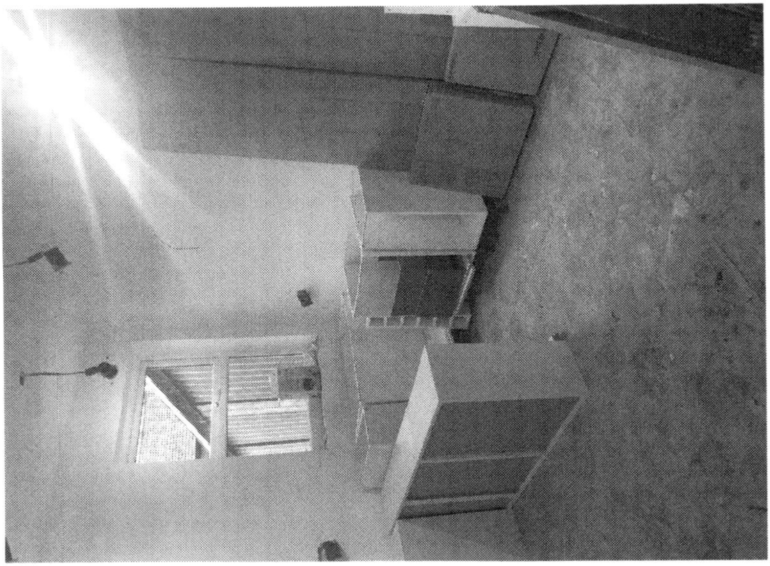

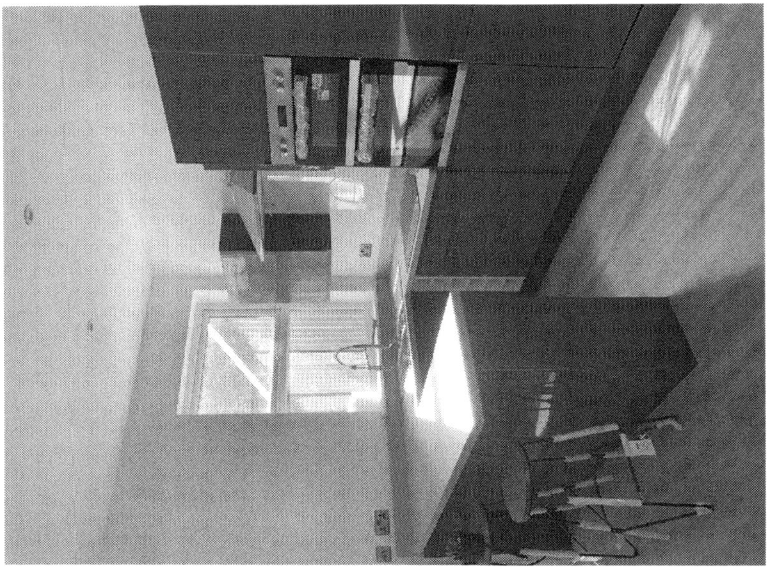

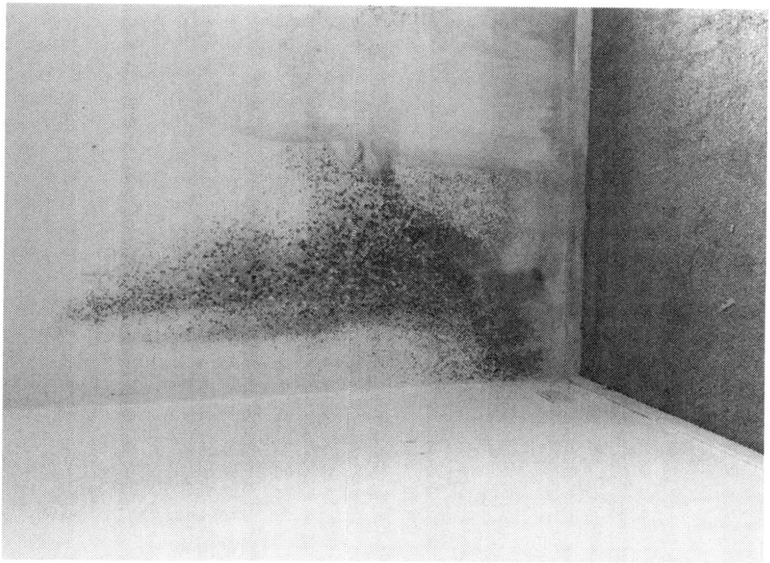

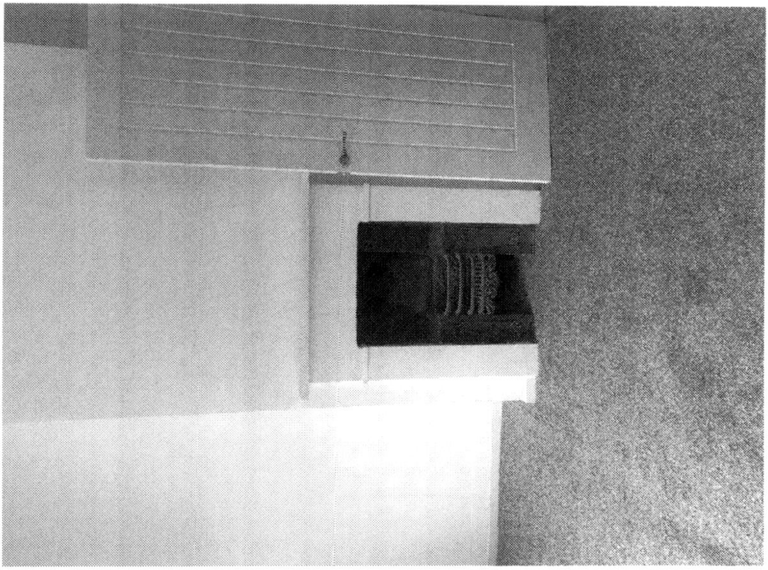

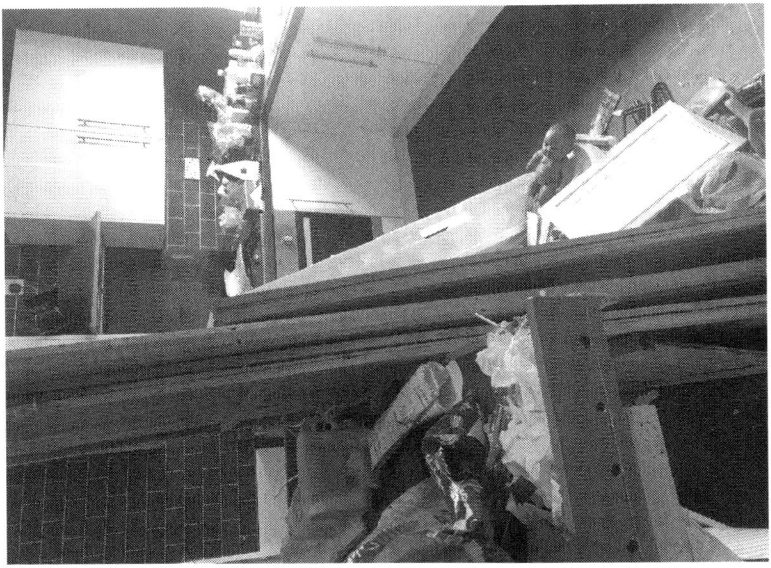

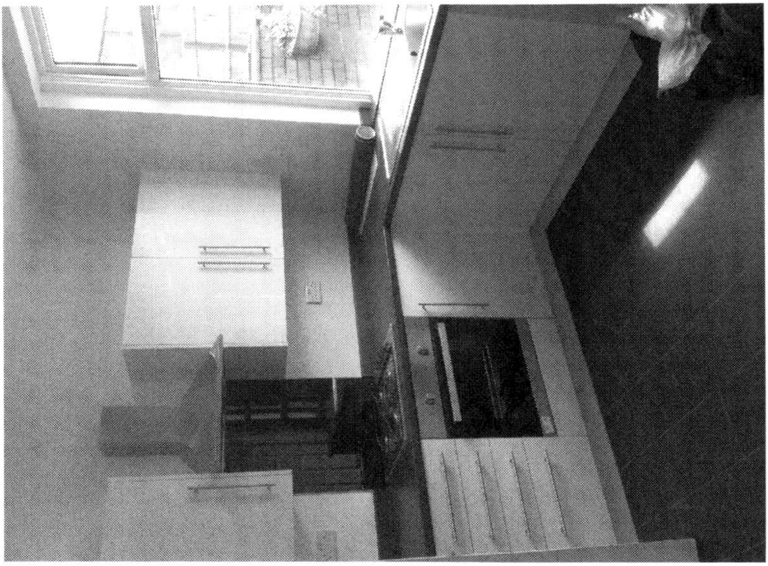

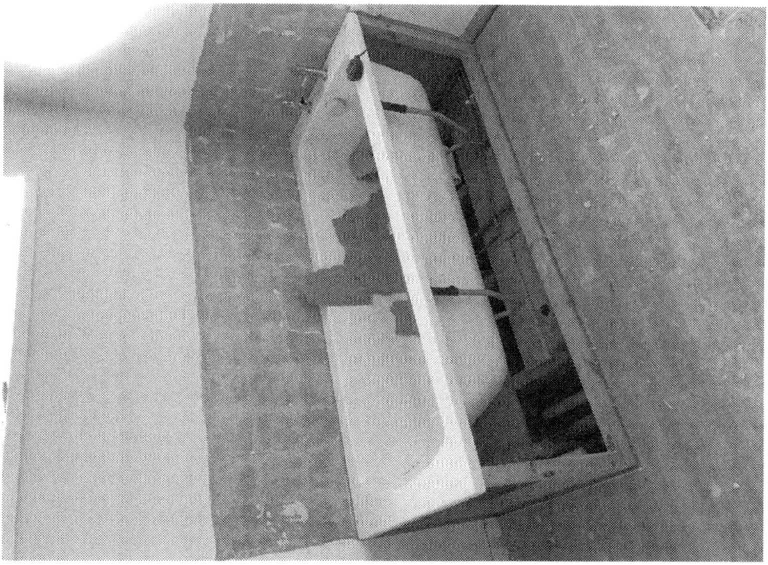

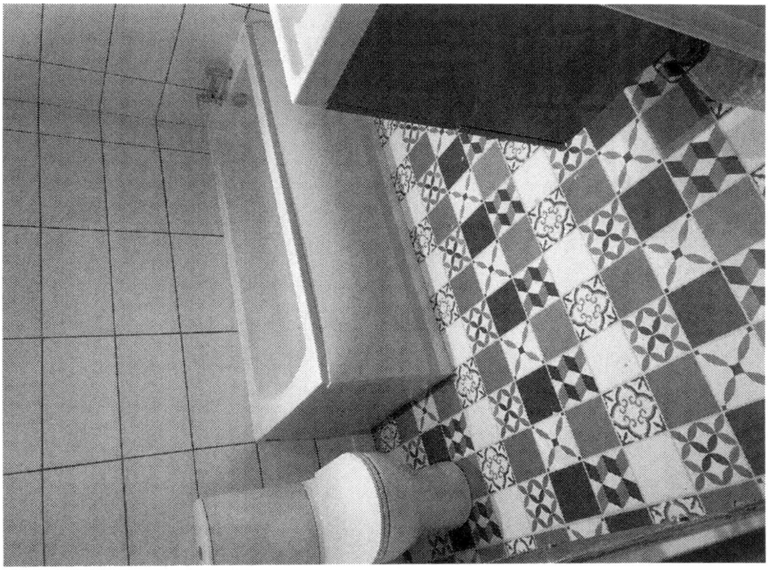

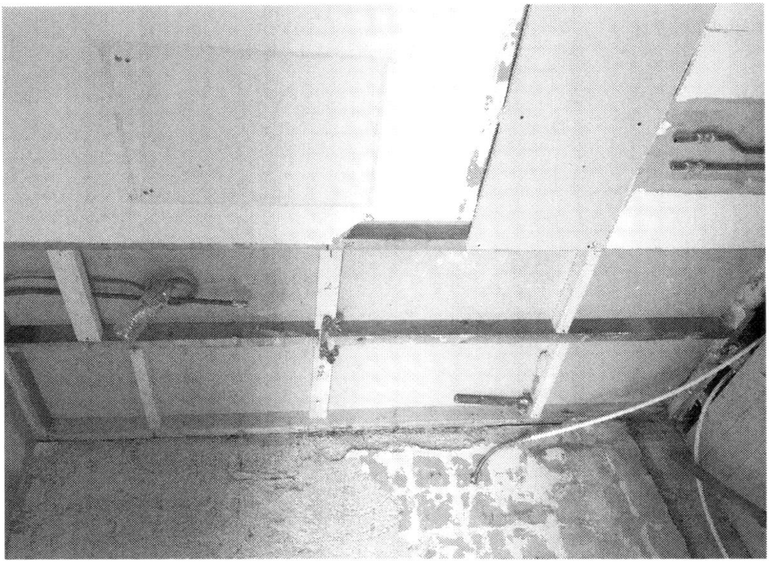

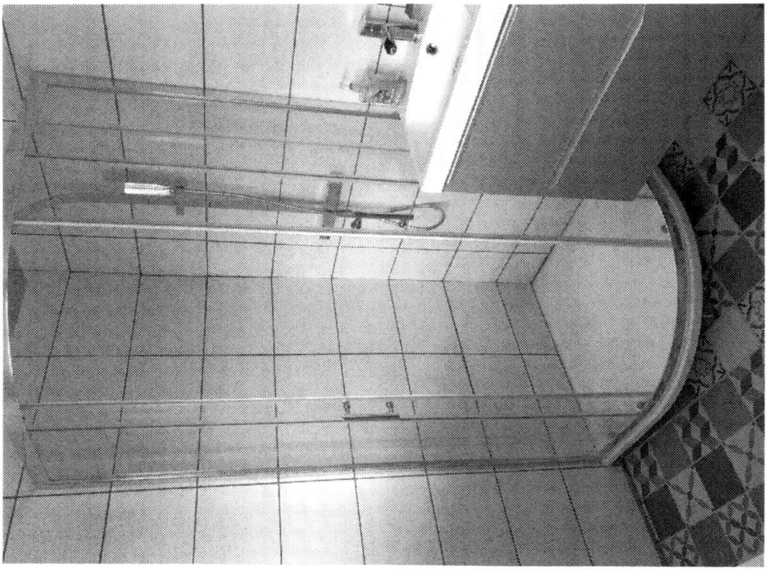

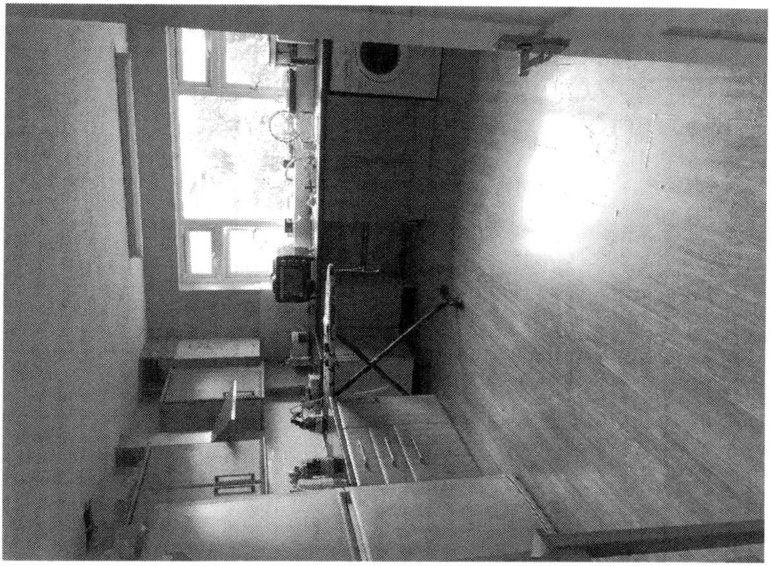

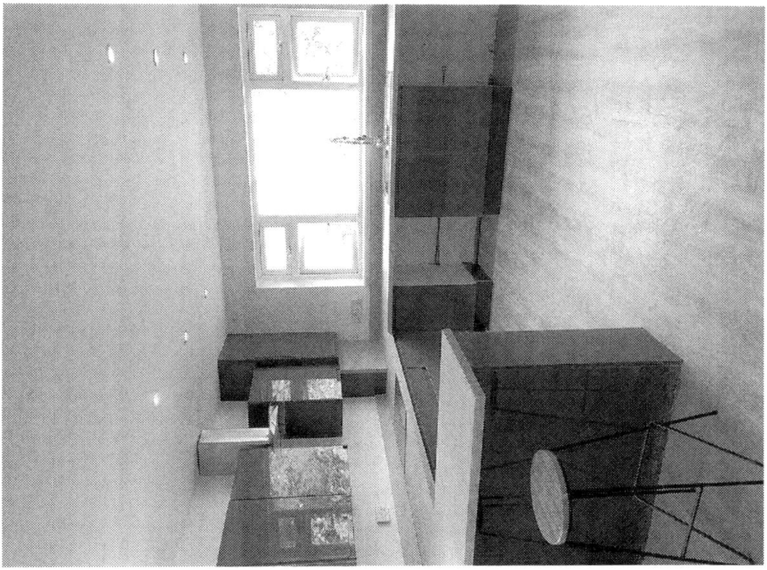

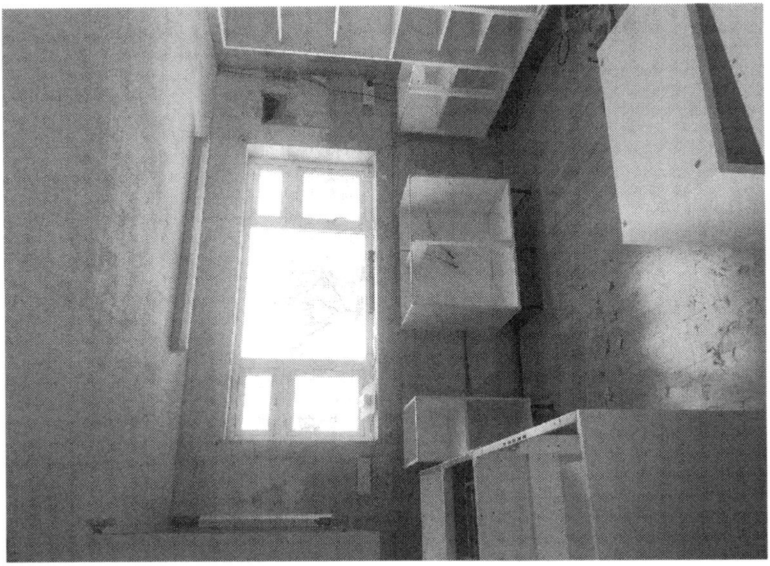

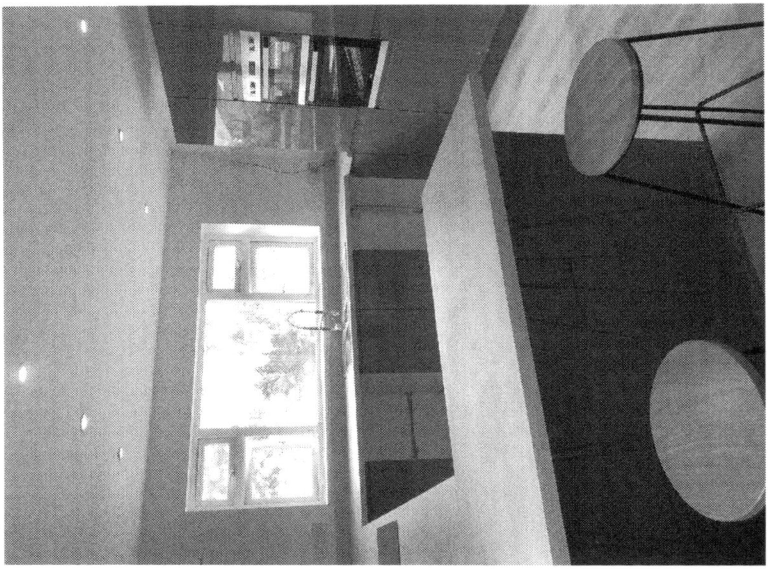

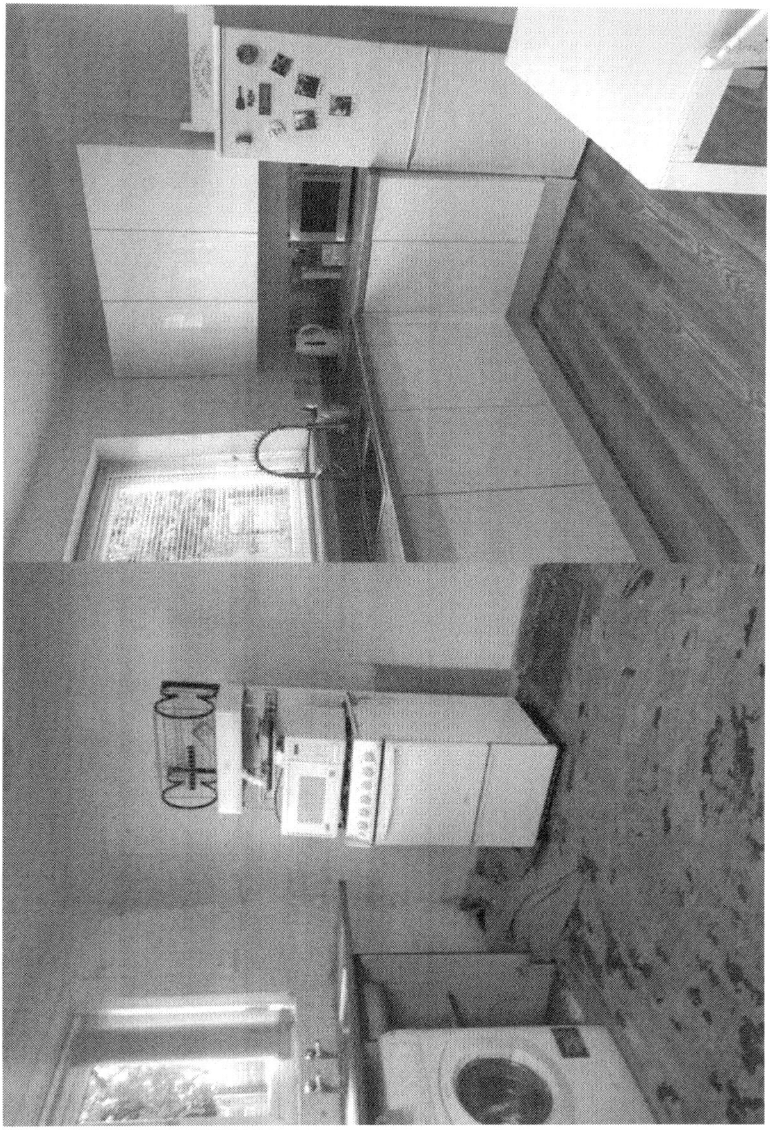

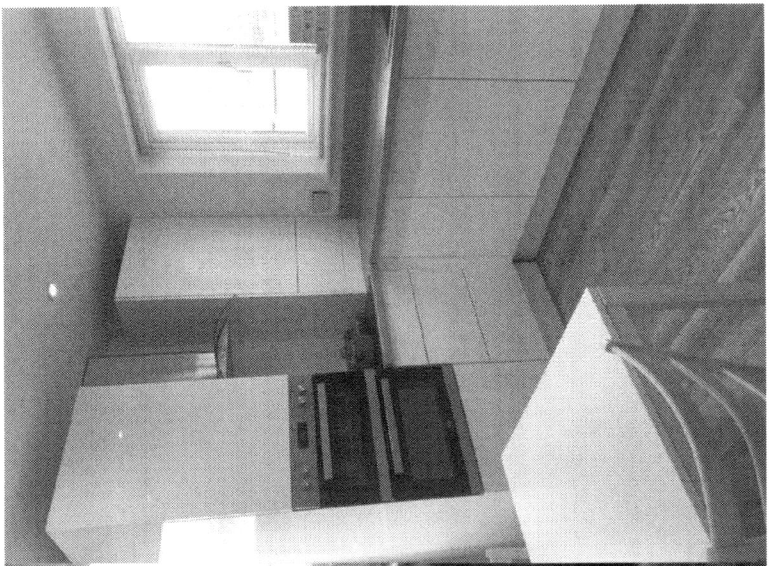

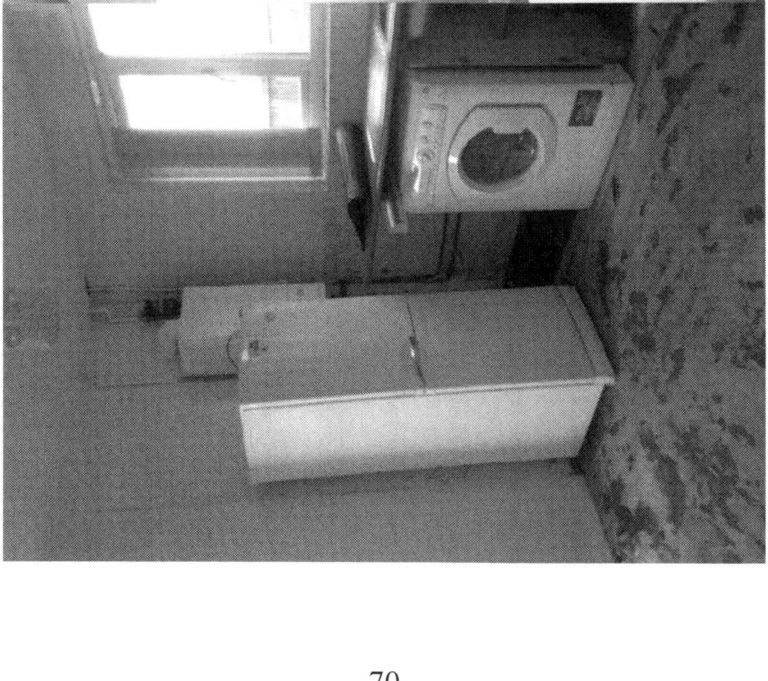

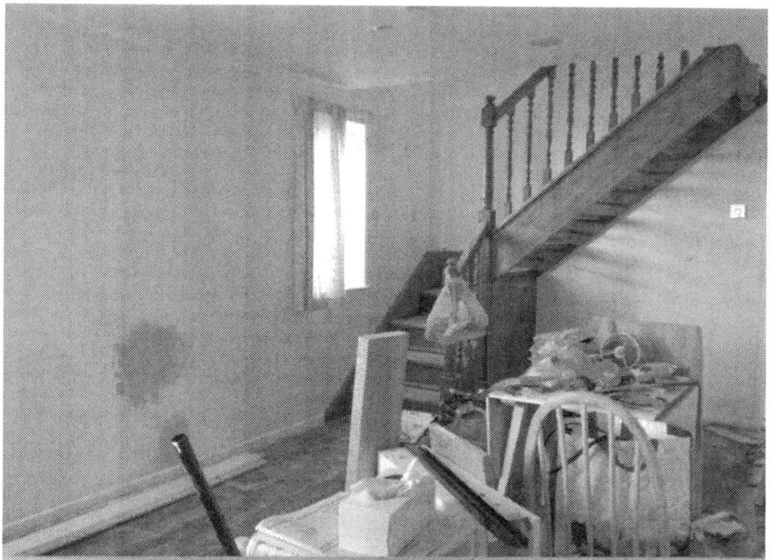
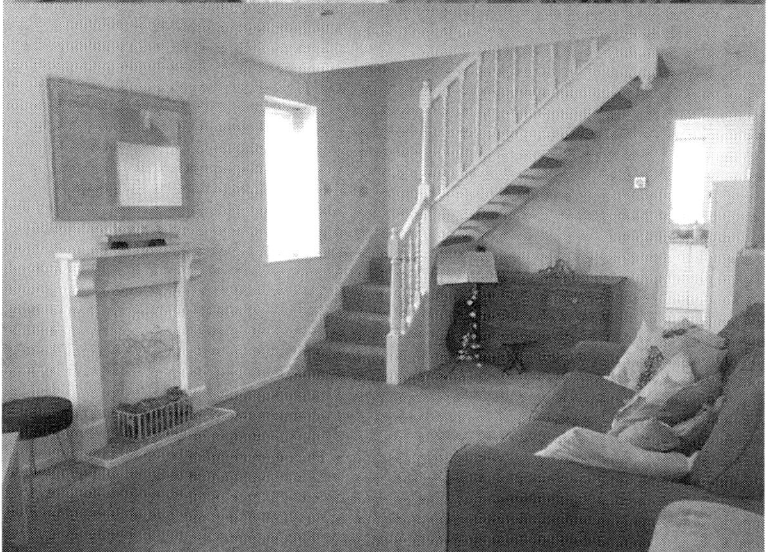

ESTIMATING COSTS

There is no way you can accurately assess the costs of any renovation by just viewing a property once or twice, without getting the whole gambit of relevant contractors and surveyors in. Even then, there is nearly always something that comes to unexpectedly bite you on the behind half way through the process. And let's face it, you are probably going to need to cost this job up roughly and without a single expert in sight after one viewing or you could lose the property to some other viewer, who has got his wits about him and knows the game inside out.

To put you in a stronger position I am going to list the works I completed while renovating a house recently and their approximate cost. This property will actually be featured soon enough as one of my three chosen case studies. This one already had double glazing and central heating, but the heating needed to be re-plumbed and there was no combi boiler. I'm going to add a couple of commonly required costs in and so you have them at your disposal. Please don't take these costs to be absolute gospel. They are based on what I can get them done for or what I've recently had to pay for them, so it is not exact but it will give you a good enough grasp of cost so you can marry them up with your findings from the viewing and an hour later have a fair idea of what you are going to offer for the property. Also, at this point in time, I did none of the work myself, so you will be able to adjust the price for anything you could do yourself.

COST ESTIMATES

Ripping out whatever is necessary.	£1000
Flat roof replaced.	£850
Rebuilding kitchen wall.	£500
4X skips.	£1000
PVCu double glazed windows X8.	£3000 (I spent £650 on a large window and door)
Gas central heating system	£4400

(Included 6 standard radiators, towel rad, vertical rad, combi boiler, first and second fixes)

Full rewire.	£2000
Plastering	£3750

(dot n dab, plasterboard some ceilings and walls, some full plastered walls, all skimmed and some wallpaper removal)

Painting.	£2500
Joinery	£1000

(Architraves, door hanging, skirting boards fitted etc)

Flooring.	£1200
Kitchen inc electric goods.	£2500
Bathroom.	£1500

(Including large vanity unit, tiles and dual rain head shower)

Extra materials and labour	£1500
(Inc kitchen fitting)	
TOTAL.	£24,350 (no VAT)

Side note: it does depend on the area and your target audience but for me it is always worth spending that little bit extra to add some higher end finishing touches where you can. Often this will only set you back £100 here and £200 there. For example, in the kitchen install a double oven or oven and microwave and a big fancy tap with spray setting; in the bathroom a rain head shower. Perhaps, fully tile the bathroom. These things won't even add up to a grand extra but they will insure you get the property rented out straight away (market willing) and when you come to sell or remortgage the property you are a hell of a lot more likely to get the valuation you want. There is a lot of competition out there!

With regards to the figures above, I'm obviously estimating. There was no real structural work involved but pretty much a full plastering job with extras and a central heating system from scratch were needed. I've done renovations that cost me £10K where I didn't even need to skim. I replaced the kitchen and bathroom, painted the already flat walls and put in new flooring; it even had a nice boiler in it. I gained about £34K of equity! It really is swings and roundabouts in this game.

MARPLE SKIP SERVICES

Telephone:
0161 427 5680
07974 286185

MINI - MIDI'S
REAR WALK-IN
8 Yard & 16 Yard

With Compliments

| 20 03 07 | Bulky waste (furniture etc) |

Chase Hazel Grove

SECTION B - WASTE PRODUCER:
B1 Name and address of company:
B2 SIC Code 2007 (TICK ONE ONLY)

NA	Householder	55.10	Hotel waste
41.20/2	Construction of domestic buildings	64.19/1	Waste from banks
41.20/1	Construction of commercial buildings	81.30	Waste from landscapers
16.29	Manufacture of wood products	82.11	Waste from offices
38.21	Waste from other waste transfer stations	84.11	Waste from council offices
43.11	Demolition waste	85.31	Waste from schools
45.20	Garage waste (motor vehicles)	47.19	Waste from shops

B3 Name and address of site to collect the waste from:
B4 Date of transfer from: Stockport Rd East Bredbury to Marple Skips
B5 I confirm that I have fulfilled my duty to apply the waste hierarchy as required by regulation 12 of the Waste (England and Wales) Regulations 2011

Date of payment

Name (print): No one on site Sign: .... Date: 28 / 1 / 2019

Date of Delivery

SECTION C - CARRIER OF WASTE:
☐ Marple Skip Services, Higher Dan Bank, Marple, Stockport SK6 7EH CB/ZP3073BD
☐ Other (give details inc. carrier's number): ....

Driver (print): Office Ken Sign: .... Date: 28 / 1 / 2019

SECTION D - WASTE DISPOSER / RECYCLER
D1 I confirm I have brought the waste to a permitted or exempt facility on behalf of the person named in section B

Name (print): .... Sign: .... Date: ....
On behalf of Marple Skip Services

D2 Name of facility:
☐ Permit EPR/GP3595VZ Dan Bank Farm ☐ Other: Permit number ....

Site address: ....
D3 I acknowledge receipt of the above waste on behalf or permit number:

Name (print): .... Sign: .... Date: ....

CUSTOMERS ORDERING VEHICLES OFF THE ROAD DO SO ENTIRELY AT THEIR OWN RISK. ANY CUSTOMER ALLOWING A FIRE IN A SKIP WILL BE CHARGED FOR THE FIRE DAMAGE. ONE-OFF SKIPS ARE HIRED FOR A 2 DAY PERIOD AND WILL BE COLLECTED UNLESS PRIOR ARRANGEMENTS HAVE BEEN MADE. CUSTOMERS OVERLOADING SKIPS ARE LIABLE TO AN EXTRA CHARGE. FOR CONDITIONS SEE REVERSE.

A3 Skips Type
☐ Mini   ☐ 14 Yard
☐ Midi   ☐ 16 yard
☑ Maxi   ☐ Other

CASH SALES ONLY
NETT £ 200 -00
VAT £ 40 -00
TOTAL £ 240 -00

SIGNING UP ON YOUR MORTGAGE

I would like to add a disclaimer between the last chapter and this: whilst all the information I have imparted to you is true to the best of my knowledge at the time of writing, lenders are constantly changing their rates and their lending criterion. They will alter the amount of background properties they will tolerate and the LTV percentages they will offer. This can be for market competitiveness or changes in governmental regulation or economic uncertainty. Often I have been to see my financial advisors, who like myself, have a current tried and trusted lender in the back of their minds, only for them to check the product details on the system and find that in the last week the lender has gone from loving portfolio landlords to hating them or they've taken 75% LTV off the table etc. So before you do anything else, always check with your FA to make sure you are still in a practical position to go ahead with a purchase.

I will cover making an offer and agreeing a sale shortly but let's briefly talk about signing up on your mortgage.

You will make an appointment for as soon as you can after your sale is agreed. You want to get the show on the road for your own sake, as time is indeed money in the property game. You also want the agent who will be monitoring and pushing your sale through, to be confident in you as a purchaser and know you are not procrastinating for all manner of reasons; namely you can't get a mortgage or you're short of cash. They will want to look like they are doing a good job for the vendor and be able to show the vendor that they can trust (that in you) they haven't chosen the wrong buyer. The Seller has the right to turn down your offer anytime up to exchange of contracts and the agent has their ear! An appointment will last anywhere from 1-1/2 hours usually and you will be required to produce: proof of identification in photo form; proof of residential address; a utility bill and 3/6 months bank statements, showing where your deposit money is coming from and that it has been in your account for at least 30 days (unless it has arrived from a solicitor for example or that it is the result of a remortgage (I will cover remortgages later on). You will also need your debit card to pay for your survey, unless your product comes with a free survey. It is also usual, at this point, to pay the first half of your FA's application fee. The second half is most likely due on completion of your purchase. You will probably be required to sign some compliance forms and such like, as well.

Once your advisor has completed and sent off your application, you will then be waiting for the valuer to be instructed by the mortgage company and subsequently waiting to receive the results of the survey he conducts. Hopefully his valuation will tally up with your figures and the agent's estimations and you will then be ready to embark on the legal side of your sale. Generally a lender will not take your survey fee until they have assessed the application. Nowadays, they won't take the money, turn down your application and not refund you, as has happened quite often in the past. Only a few years ago, buyers were being warned that the valuation fee was non-refundable and that they might lose it. I have been the victim of this but I luckily got a refund on appeal. Also FYI most BTL lenders will only deal with an advisor i.e. you can't apply directly to the lender and avoid the FA's fees.

I will come to adverse survey issues in good time. You will not progress to the legal side of your purchase until you have ironed out any problems that have arisen as a result of the survey. You don't want to start paying out more money if the sale can't be negotiated past this point.

the mortgage works
common sense lending

Confirmation of Gifted Deposit

Please complete this form in black ink and in block capitals

Mortgage Customer Details

Customer's name(s)	
Customer's current address including postcode	, HAZEL GROVE, STOCKPORT Postcode: SK7
Security address of property to be purchased	GRUNDY STREET, HAZEL GROVE, STOCKPORT Postcode: SK7 4EU

Donor Details

Donor's full name(s):	
Donor's residential address including postcode	REDDISH, STOCKPORT Postcode: SK5
Donor's telephone contact number(s):	
Relationship to the above mortgage customer(s):	FATHER IN-LAW
Amount of the gift	£34,395
If the gifted amount exceeds the deposit amount please provide an explanation	

Declaration

I/We confirm that the deposit is an unconditional and non-refundable gift and I/We will have no rights or interest in the property whatsoever.
I/We understand that I/We may be asked for proof that I/We have the deposit monies available.
I/We do not intend to reside in the property. I/We understand the importance of seeking independent legal advice and have had the opportunity to do so
I/We understand that my/our personal documentation provided to support this application (gifted deposit) will be held, with all other information relating to this mortgage application. The original documentation will be returned as soon as possible. If the mortgage applicant(s) requests a copy of their mortgage application file now or at any point in the future, the personal information I/We have provided may be included in the information that you provide to them.

Donor(s) signature(s):

Date 06/09/2016

Please refer to 'Source of Deposit' section of Lending Guide for supporting proofs required

MAKING AN OFFER

Now it is time to consider your offer. There is more than one mechanism the agent may use to accept an offer. The usual process being that you put the offer to the agent and the agent puts the offer in turn to the vendor and awaits the vendor's instructions. The offer can also take the form of best and final bids whereupon the agent gives a deadline for the interested parties to put in their maximum bid and any conditions or benefits incumbent on it. Examples include: the offer being subject to survey or not, promises of timescales, method of payment (cash or mortgage etc) and more besides. Sealed bids is similar but the offers are all opened at the same time on the offering deadline. Even though people tow the line with these rules, the vendor can still change their mind and if for instance you are not the winning bidder, if you still want to up your bid, then the estate agent is legally obliged to put it forward, unless the vendor has specifically requested otherwise. It's essentially a tidier way of taking offers for a property that is likely to receive an abundance of interest. This is usually due to its desirability based on a good potential profit margin. With all these methods, your offer is never disclosed to any other party; only the vendor.

AUCTION

Auction is different. A catalogue of properties are offered for sale one at a time by an auctioneer and the bids are in a public arena (domain) so everyone is aware of the state of play at any given moment. Each property will have a guide price to give some indication of the ball park figure you are expected to start bidding at. You can even proxy bid on line or via a representative on the phone. The winner is essentially the last person standing and on the fall of the hammer they have exchanged contracts and are given 28 days to complete. If they fail to complete on time then they leave themselves open to legal repercussions. Sometimes the bidding doesn't reach the reserve price. The reserve is the minimum price the vendor is willing to accept and this is an undisclosed figure but usually within about 10% of the guide price. When this happens the auctioneer will invite the bidders to approach the administration team on site to see if a deal can be worked out. If it can, a normal sale will then take place.

There is a similar style of auction that takes place on line. Essentially there is a deadline again for all bids to be in and again you can see a list of the bids as well as the current highest bidder. There is also a reserve and a guide price associated with this.

On top of this is the 'Modern Method of Auction'. It is the same process as the others but there is an additional (usually fairly large) fee associated with the sale price and this is a deposit that you lose if you pull out of the sale ie no legal repercussions. For this fee you have the privilege of a lengthier completion deadline, eg 56 days, which makes it easier to obtain a mortgage within the timescale.

In most cases with auctions, the vendors are amenable to agreeing a sale by normal methods, prior to the auction taking place.

We will assume here that you are offering on the property

the normal way ie you view the house, you like it, you call the agent, make an offer and await the vendor's decision. Offering the asking price may secure you the property straight away and will show that you are a serious buyer. However, It could make the vendor think that they have marketed the house at too low a price and they might hold out for more interest if the property has just come on the market. In most cases you would begin your bidding at a lower price and increase the offers gradually, in the hope that you will agree a sale at a cheaper price. There has always been a perceived rule (not just for houses) that you offer three times and the vendor will consider your third bid to be the last. Whether this is intentional or was ever a real thing is open to question but there are actually no hard and fast rules to offering. In most cases I would certainly start low and increase the offer gradually but that depends if you can suss out the competition accurately. If on the viewing the house is full of other viewers ie. you are on a block viewing, you may be wise to jump right in with the asking price and be ready for it to go above, if there is money to be made.

Block viewings are made to save the agents time where the agent suspects a house will garner a lot of interest, usually where there is a profit to be made. Not only does it save the agent from doing a lot of separate viewings but if there are several viewers at an appointment, it makes the house seem more popular and drum up more interest faster; similar to auction fever. When arranging the viewing, you can always ask the agent how much interest there has been eg. how many viewings there have been and how many are booked in for the future. You can even enquire if any offers have been put in. The agent will often tell you if anyone has offered and if the offer has been accepted or not but will not tell you the actual figure, as that is against the law. If they have only had offers that have been rejected then they may hint around the highest unacceptable offer by advising you that you need to be offering over a certain figure. In my opinion this is good form. Even if they told you the figure, it really only serves to give you a base to start from and saves everyone time, instead of you starting unbeknownst £5K lower and working your way up. Some agents won't give you any information and bang on about the law instead of helping their vendor by oiling the wheels of the process and that I find frustrating and pointless. You know who you are; grow up!

Also be prepared for the fact that however well you prepare yourself and to some degree, how much you offer, you won't always get the result you hoped for.

BRIDGING FINANCE

Bridging loans are sometimes a faster way to get the finance you need. They are also the correct way to purchase a property, be it residential or commercial that is being purchased to renovate and flip; (if you don't have entirely cash purchasing power that is.) There are other products called Commercial Mortgages for purchasing commercial properties such as, shops, units, factories etc (anything not entirely residential), but as my knowledge of them is limited I will omit them from this guide book. You can even get agricultural mortgages that specialise in farms, land and equestrian facilities. Again I have only flirted with such projects and don't know enough to responsibly impart any knowledge about them. Bridging loans can be used in residential purchases to 'bridge' the gap between purchases whilst arranging long term finance. I will give an example in one of the case studies featuring one of my own projects later in the book.

Bridging finance is also used when purchasing land to build new property on. There are many combinations of repayment but following your application being approved, which includes many things such as: architects plans, structural engineers reports, details of your construction company and theirs / your own experience in the trade and a myriad other hurdles to jump. You put down eg 50% of the land price and 10% of each tranche (stage of building) of the project. The interest can sometimes be 'back ended' so you can pay less money monthly as your project progresses. Usually these tranches are sectioned into foundations, first floor, second floor and roof. They release money at the start of each stage so you can finance the build. Once the properties are complete or a legitimate stage is, you sell or remortgage them to pay off part or all of your bridge. This then brings the payments down as you are lending less. Bridges always require an exit plan.

Why wouldn't everyone use this easy way of financing projects? The short answer is it's expensive! You will pay a much higher interest rate which is calculated monthly. You also have an entrance fee and sometimes an exit fee. These fees amount to a lot more than the fees and interest rates you will become accustomed to in the mortgage arena.

Auction finance is a form of bridging loan and is designed to purchase within the strict timescales of buying at auction. It is possible to use a mortgage lender but the time it takes to wade through the mortgage process can vary greatly. So you can't always rely on a mortgage product to facilitate an auction purchase. Although you could apply for both facilities and choose your preferred method at the time (credit score and criterion permitting). The one time when I needed auction finance (and I'm sure it won't be the last) my fees were this:

2% entrance fee
1% exit fee
0.49% monthly interest rate for 6 months
1.24% monthly interest rate for the remaining 6 months of the 12 month term
There were other administration fees involved as there are

with mortgages that I haven't included but they are nominal in comparison.

I borrowed 75% of £85,000 i.e. £63,750 so my monthly fees for the first 6 months were approximately £350 per month and £790 per month for the final 6 months.

My original exit plan was to sell the property but the market for selling proved to be in a little bit of a slump at the time, so I remortgaged it on a BTL product and rented it out. I didn't get my full profit out but I got most of it and the rest is tied up in the equity I have sitting in the property.

together.

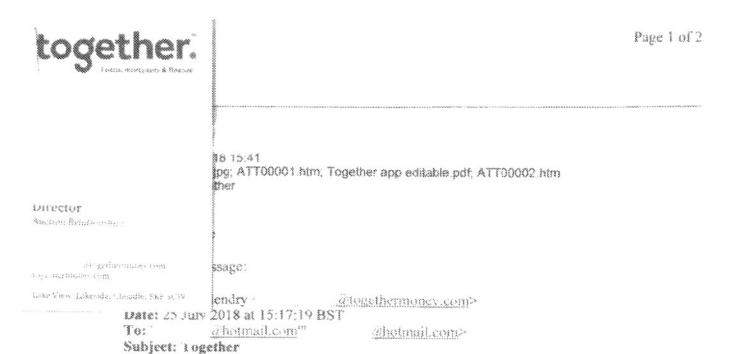

Director

Date: 25 July 2018 at 15:17:19 BST
To: @hotmail.com
Subject: Together

Nice to speak to you earlier.

In summary we are able to provide funding within very short timescales and many of our completions are funded within just 5 working days. We can lend on any type of property in any condition whether bought via auction, estate agent or even privately.

We specialize in short term finance up to a term of 12 month, although this can be redeemed at any time, therefore allowing you the ability to purchase the property quickly and sufficient time to either remortgage or sell. The facility can be settled at any time as there is no minimum period.

Typical LTV would be up to 75% of purchase price on residential investment. 100% finance is available subject to the inclusion of additional property with suitable levels of equity on a 1st or 2nd Legal Charge (usually up to 70% of valuation minus existing mortgage if applicable)

The product details are as follows;

6 month Resi product (minimum loan £30,000)
* 2% fee (min £995)
* 0.49% per month (rate will increase to 1.24% after 6 months)
* 2% exit fee

Or

12 month product for Resi loans (min loan £50,000 - £100,000)
* 2% fee
* 0.9% per month
* one month exit

All the above would be subject to a Title Indemnity fee from £100. In addition there may also be a possibility of no lenders legal fees or valuation, of course this together with all other fees stated can be determined upon a full case review.

To complete the application form please refer to the attached

25/07/2018

together.

Loans, mortgages & finance.

Accountant's certificate

Details

Client name			
Company name	HAZELWOOD LAUNDRY	Company registration number	N/A
Business address	16 HAZELWOOD ROAD	Nature of business	LAUNDRY SERVICES
Business postcode	SK7 4LE	Business trading for 13 years ___ months	
Business email	hazelwoodlaundry@ntlworld.com	Client's share of business %	100
Business phone	0161 483 0671	Accounting year end	31 MARCH
Incorporation status:	Sole Trader ✓ Partnership ☐ Limited Company ☐ Other (please state)		

	This Year Projection (Uncertified)	This Year to Date (Uncertified)	Last Year (Certified)	2 Years Ago (Certified)
For the Business:				
Year end date				
Turnover / gross income	See separate sheet attached			
P/it after tax				
Dividends paid				
For the Client:				
Gross salary				
Net salary (after tax & N.I.)				
Dividends received				
Other income				
Total net income				

Additional information

Accountant details

Name of company	IN ACCOUNTANCY LTD	Accountant's name	
Business phone	0161 456 9666	Practising certificate valid until	04 2019

Possess one of the following qualifications:
- Institute of Chartered Accountants in England and Wales (ACA/FCA)
- Institute of Chartered Accountants in Scotland (CA)
- Association of Chartered Certified Accountants (ACCA/FCCA)
- Association of Accounting Technicians (MAAT/FMAAT)
- Chartered Institute of Management Accountants (ACMA/FCMA)
- Institute of Financial Accountants (AFA/FFA)
- Association of Authorised Public Accountants (AAPA/FAPA)
- Association of International Accountants (AAIA/FAIA)
- Certified Public Accountants Association (ACPA/FCPA)
- Chartered Institute of Taxation (CTA)

Member reference	7478276		
We have acted for the applicant for 0 years 1 months		Business email	@in-accountancy.co.uk
How were you introduced to the client? CLIENT CONTACTED US			

Confirmation & signature

I/We confirm by my/our signature below that:
- ✓ We have obtained details from the business named above of all bank accounts kept, maintained or operated by the business during the accounting period noted above.
- ✓ We have examined the business' book-keeping system and in my/our opinion adequate records are kept of all transactions relating to business activities.
- ✓ We declare that our client is solvent and trading and able to pay their debts within the meaning of the Insolvency Act 1986.
- ✓ We declare that we know of no material issues that may affect the sustainability of the income being declared for the business or client detailed above.

Date	14/8/2018	Company Stamp	N/A
Signature			

BRO002.2   ON BEHALF OF IN ACCOUNTANCY LTD

SALE AGREED

Let us assume that your offer has been accepted. You want to get the wheels in motion as quickly as you can; especially if this was after a block viewing. The vendor will be advised that they have reserve offers if you start procrastinating. The vendor is less likely to switch buyers if you can demonstrate that you are proactive.

So your first move is to arrange an appointment with your FA and advise the agent that you have done so. This appointment should take between 1 and 2 hours. You will most likely be asked to take documentation such as: photo ID, proof of address, 3 months bank statements and your last 3 months wage slips / 2-3 year's SA302s if you are self employed. There will also be a few extra forms to fill in eg compliance. They will also want proof of your funds i.e. proof of your deposit and this will need to have been in your account for more than 30 days. You may be exempt from this if the money you are using is via a gifted deposit (a gift from a relative will need to be accompanied by the necessary signed form to confirm as much and they will have to go through the same vetting of proof that you would have done), or the money has been deposited in your account by a solicitor as a result of a property or business sale or a remortgage.

The advisor will run through the available product options and accompanied by your criterion, help you decide on the best product for you taking into account the following:

LTV
Fixed rate and duration
Rate of interest
Arrangement fee
Redemption penalty
Further advance period / fees
Length of entire loan
Interest only or repayment
Survey

Side note: if you are planning to rent the property out long term and its contribution to your pension is of the utmost concern ie the immediate income isn't: you may for example choose a 65% LTV, 10 year fixed rate, repayment mortgage. You can own the property out right in eg 25 years.

You may require this property to provide a larger portion of your current income. Interest rates may be fairly low and stable, and you might want to remortgage the property in a couple of years to free up some equity with a view to reinvesting it in more property in the future. In this case you may want to opt for a 75% LTV, 2 year fixed rate, interest only deal. I hasten to add that these are only rough examples and you should always take qualified advice from a professional; as I always do!

You also need to instruct a solicitor. The cheapest is not always the best choice and you would be wise to take recommendation from your FA and the estate agency; the latter especially. The agent will be dealing with solicitors day in and day out in the process of 'chasing' yours and everyone else's sales. They will know which solicitors sit back and who the proactive ones are. They will also know who specialises in Conveyancing (property law) and more importantly who answers the phone when they call. A good conveyancer will be set up so as to be able to cope with an influx of agents asking for updates on particular cases. In my opinion you should steer away from the call centre type solicitors and focus on the local firms. You are more likely to speak to the same person when you or the agent calls and they will be more involved, personally, in your case. Plus the smaller firms are more likely to be hungry for the business. Internet based agents seem to use exactly the sort of solicitors I've just warned you about (in my experience) and so I would advise you to go your own way. Naming no names, when I was an agent for Reeds Rains there was a firm local to myself who had a couple of solicitors dealing with the Conveyancing and an excellent legal secretary who was on the ball and was abreast of all of the cases. Equally, I was on top of maybe 90 sales files without needing to even look at them. I would call the secretary up with 1, 3, 7 files to chase and she would call me back in an hour with all the information. This saved us both a lot of time and therefore we recommended their firm every time to our prospective purchasers. In fairly recent times they have become more and more corporate and the service and experience is not fantastic in my opinion. But as with anything else, there are always exceptions to the rule. Solicitors will also require proof of identification and funds and require various forms to be completed.

Now you have two concurrent avenues to pursue: the mortgage side and the legal side. Once these are both satisfied then you can progress to an exchange of contracts, which means both parties are legally bound to the sale. Their solicitor will have requested your deposit fund, which prior to this must have been received by your solicitor. Then you have completion, whereupon monies are exchanged and fees are settled via solicitors. At this point you are now the legal owner of the property. Let us consider the stages of the process that have brought us to this point.

MORTGAGE SIDE

Agreement in principle
Application sent for approval (continuous process)
Application pre approved
Valuation instructed
Valuation report / survey results received by lender
Valuation assessed
Underwriters complete assessment of all documents
Application approved
Mortgage offer released

On the other side of the transaction the legal process will be running concurrently.

LEGAL SIDE

Vendor's solicitor requests details from the vendor.
Vendor's solicitor requests copy of deeds and office copies of the leasehold.

Vendor's solicitor receives information requested.

Vendor's solicitor compiles and issues a draft contract of sale to your solicitor.

Purchaser's solicitor sends off the searches (local, water, drainage, debt and various others eg coal mining usually). These take 2-5 weeks on the whole but generally closer to 2, depending on the council involved and their backlog.

Purchaser's solicitor raises any enquiries with the vendor's solicitor regarding points in the contract they want clarifying or altering.

Vendor's solicitor replies to enquiries (these last two stages continue almost interminably it seems and they are usually hung up on the leaseholder that no one can find, and you end up getting indemnity insurance to cover these issues anyway).

Purchaser's solicitor receives the results of the searches (rarely unsatisfactory).

Purchaser's solicitor receives the mortgage offer.

Purchaser's solicitor receives satisfactory replies to enquiries.

To summarise: Searches in, mortgage offer in, enquiries in; it's time for exchange and completion. Incidentally this process takes around 6-8 weeks on average so be prepared to wait. The galling thing about this is: on a course I did with an estate agent, the course leader regaled the time he managed (by going between all parties and indeed the mortgage company on foot and in car) got the whole sales process done in 24 hours! He told us the anecdote to emphasise how much unnecessary 'effing around all these people do.

The exchange date will be decided on between yourself and the vendor, communicated between the solicitors and mediated by the estate agent. What a palaver!

This is by no means an exhaustive list; this is the process running smoothly! There are several things that can intervene in the sale's process e.g. The rental value doesn't tally up with the property value and the lender decides that they need extra deposit from you (a disproportionate amount it seems). The solicitor as mentioned previously, can't find the leaseholder and they waste an age trying to find them before reaching the inevitable indemnity insurance solution. Something adverse appears on one of the searches e.g. there is a historic coal mining air shaft under the property. The property boundaries aren't defined or in one case I was a part of, the owners of a 2 bed terraced didn't actually own the piffling little yard they were advertising as part of the property; this caused the solicitor and lender issues.

So now you have your exchange and completion date, you've paid your deposit, set up your buildings insurance to start on exchange and the lender has confirmed to the solicitor that they will release the moneys for said completion date.

You exchange, complete and the house is now yours.

Side note: The vendor may give permission for a key undertaking to allow you to do works (usually only works that are a condition of the mortgage and usually only for residential purchasers) between exchange and completion. It's worth an ask to get a head start. The more work you can get done while you are not paying for the mortgage the better.

Reeds Rains

iamsold

6th Floor, Arden House, Regent Centre,
Newcastle upon Tyne, Tyne and Wear, NE3 3LU
Tel: 0808 208 4294
Email: completions@iamsold.co.uk

Date: 23/05/2019

Notification Of Sale by Auction for: Street, Hazel Grove, Stockport, SK7

Sale Price: £125,000.00

Auction Pack: https://www.reedsrainsauction.co.uk/properties/SK_____/auction-pack?si=19029498155861   Residential Auction Pack

Vendor:	Mr Jeremy Corporation Road, Workington Cumbria County ca12
Vendor Solicitor:	Keoghs Nicholls Lindsell & Harris Miss 8-10 Commercial Road Hazel Grove Stockport Greater Manchester SK7 4AA **Tel:** / **Email:** @keoghssolicitors.co.uk
Purchaser(s):	Mr & Mr Close; Grosvenor Street Hazel Grove Stockport Greater Manchester SK7 ;SK7
Purchaser Solicitor:	SAS Daniels LLP Miss 30 Greek Street Mountbatten Way Stockport Chesire SK3 8AD **Tel:** 0161 475 7600 **Email:** @sasdaniels.co.uk

the mortgage works
common sense lending

REPORT AND VALUATION FOR MORTGAGE

APPLICANT'S COPY
Date of Inspection: 05/08/2015
Reference: 000001204

NAME OF APPLICANT Mr
PROPERTY Road, Poynton, Stockport, Cheshire, SK12

1. DESCRIPTION: End terrace house
Year of construction (approx.) 1910

2. NEW PROPERTIES:
Is builder registered with NHBC/Zurich? No
Stage Reached
Is inspection required? no

3. TENURE
Freehold Unexpired Lease 0 Years Ground Rent £ 0 pa Maintenance £ pa

4. ACCOMMODATION (Indicate No. of rooms, etc.)

Floors	Reception Rooms	Kitchens(s)	Bedrooms	Bathroom(s)	Internal W.C.s	Other Rooms	Garage/Space	Outbuildings
2	2	1	2	1	2		Unknown	0

5. SERVICES (Not Tested)

Electricity	Gas	Main Drainage	Main Water	Central Heating	Hot Water System	Satisfactory Sanitary Arrangements	Is the access satisfactory?
yes	yes	yes	yes	Gas	yes	yes	yes

6. CONSTRUCTION
primary secondary
a) External Walls Brick
b) Roof Slate
c) Garage None, None

7. REPAIRS / ESSENTIAL REPORTS:
No specialist reports required for mortgage purposes.

8. INSURANCE
Full Reinstatement Value £ 110,000 External Floor Area 94 m²

Yes / No
(a) Is the property in an area that (to the best of your knowledge) has suffered flooding or is at risk of flooding? — no
(b) Is there any indication of or any reason to anticipate structural damage arising from subsidence, landslip or heave? — no
(c) Are you aware of any subsidence, landslip or heave in the immediate vicinity? — no
(d) Are there any special risks to be considered e.g. the position, exposure, condition of the property or previous losses which could influence an insurer in its acceptance of the property for Insurance cover? — no

(If the answer to any of these four questions is 'YES' please give full details and recommendations below)

9. LEGAL REQUIREMENTS
Conveyancer to confirm the appropriate rights of way and management arrangements are in existence for the shared access to the rear of the property.

the mortgage works

REPORT AND VALUATION FOR MORTGAGE

APPLICANT'S COPY
Date of inspection: 05/06/2015
Reference: 00000120

NAME OF APPLICANT	Mr
PROPERTY	Road, Poynton, Stockport, Cheshire, SK12

10. OBSERVATIONS

Elements of the property appear to be in poor condition having regard to its age and construction. Work of repair, maintenance and renewal are required. Valuations undertaken by this firm are administered and processed centrally; the inspection and report have however been carried out by a local surveyor with good local knowledge. Distance to property 18 miles. The location of the property provides reasonable access for most usual local amenities. On the day of the inspection the local property market was buoyant. The property will be considered suitable for mortgage purposes subject to repair that is required. The property be suitable for immediate letting once the works have been completed. Checks have not been carried out to ensure the property meets statutory letting requirements. This is an amended report in pursuance of specialist reports.

Note: This report has been prepared solely for TMW purposes. It is not a structural report and is based upon a limited inspection. It may not reveal serious defects and may contain inaccuracies and omissions. It is unlikely to be adequate for purchasers' purposes and should not be relied upon. You are strongly advised to obtain a fuller report on the property.

11. VALUATION FOR MORTGAGE PURPOSES based on Full vacant possession

(a) In present condition	£165,000	(b) After completion of essential work	£165,000

12. MORTGAGE CLASSIFICATION

If past commercial use, is the residential use LESS THAN 40%   n/a

13. RENTAL ASSESSMENT

Current Rental Income	£0	Estimated rental income: £725	Demand for Letting	Steady

14. CERTIFICATE

The property is suitable security for mortgage purposes

the mortgage works

The Mortgage Works (UK) plc
Service Centre Lending
Portman House
Richmond Hill
Bournemouth
Dorset
BH2 6EP

Date: 10 June 2019	Reference: 1689
	Please quote this reference in all correspondence.

Your mortgage offer

Applicant(s)	Our Conveyancer(s)
	SAS Daniels LLP
	30 Greek Street
	Stockport
	Cheshire
	SK3 8AD

We are pleased to offer you a loan on the following basis. Please contact us if you would like an explanation of any of the terms of this mortgage offer. Please see Section 14.

This offer is valid for 6 months from the date shown on this offer. You are free to decline this offer, but you would lose any fees that you have already paid.

EARLIER MORTGAGE OFFERS

This Mortgage Offer replaces any earlier Mortgage Offer we have made you on this property.

Details of the Property to be mortgaged:

Address:	Vine Street, Hazel Grove, STOCKPORT, Cheshire, SK7
Tenure:	Freehold
Property Type:	Semi Detached House
Mortgage Type:	House Purchase - Buy to Let

1. About this offer document

- You are not bound by the terms of this offer document until you have signed the Mortgage Deed and the funds for the mortgage are released

- You should compare this offer document with the illustration given to you before you applied for this mortgage, to see how the details may have changed.

2. Which service were you provided with?

☑ TIME Mortgage Experts Ltd recommended that you take out this mortgage.

☐ TIME Mortgage Experts Ltd did not recommend a particular mortgage for you. You must make your own choice whether to accept this mortgage offer.

If you have any queries about the service you were provided with, you should contact TIME Mortgage Experts Ltd. The Mortgage Works (UK) plc is not responsible for the advice or information you have received.

3. Your mortgage requirements

This offer is based on the following mortgage requirements:

- A mortgage of £93,750.00 plus £995.00 for fees that will be added to the loan. These and the additional fees that you need to pay are shown in Section 8
- The purchase price of the property is £125,000.00
- You require the mortgage over a term of 30 years
- You require the mortgage on an interest-only basis

Changes to any of the information you have given us could alter the details in this offer. If this is the case we may provide you with a revised offer or in some cases we may need to reconsider your application.

4. Description of this mortgage

Mortgage lender: The Mortgage Works (UK) plc

Mortgage product: 5 Year Fixed BTL B90829

A fixed rate of 2.49% until 31st July 2024, followed by The Mortgage Works (UK) plc Managed Variable Rate (Issue 7), currently 5.24%, for the remaining term of the mortgage. The Managed Variable Rate is not linked to the Bank of England base rate and is not subject to any upper limit or cap.

Major product restrictions

The maximum loan allowed for this product is £1,500,000. The property must be in England, Wales or mainland Scotland.

5. Overall cost of this mortgage

The overall cost takes into account the payments in Sections 6 and 8 below. However, it excludes any payments that you may need to make into a separate savings plan to build up a lump sum to repay the amount borrowed, but assumes that you pay off the amount borrowed as a lump sum at the end of the mortgage.

The annual percentage rate of charge (APRC) is the total cost of the mortgage expressed as an annual percentage of the total amount of credit. The APRC is provided to help you compare different illustrations.

The total amount you must pay back, including the amount borrowed is	£231,545.37
This means you pay back	£2.44 for every £1 borrowed
The APRC applicable for your mortgage is	4.7% APRC

The figures in this section will vary following interest rate changes and if you do not keep the mortgage for 30 years.

Only use the figures in this section to compare the cost with another interest-only mortgage.

This APRC is calculated using assumptions regarding the interest rate. Because part of your mortgage is a variable interest rate mortgage, the actual APRC could be different from this APRC if the interest rate for your mortgage changes. For example, if the interest rate rose to 10.49%, the APRC could increase to 11.3%.

6. What you will need to pay each month — Monthly payments

This offer is based on a mortgage of £94,745.00 and includes the fees that are shown in Section 8 as being added to your mortgage and assumes that the mortgage will start on 1 July 2019.

1 payment at a fixed rate of 2.49%
followed by £396.97

59 payments at a fixed rate of 2.49%
followed by £196.60

300 payments at a variable rate, currently 5.24%
£413.73

Your first payment will be different from subsequent amounts, because in addition to the first full monthly payment it includes the accrued interest due from the day the money was released.

Cost of repaying the capital

The monthly payments shown above cover only the interest and not the capital borrowed. At the end of the mortgage term, you will still owe £94,745.00. You have advised us that you intend to sell your second investment property upon maturity of this mortgage term which will have sufficient value to repay the full capital balance outstanding under this mortgage.

It is important that you check regularly that your repayment strategy is on track to repay this mortgage at the end of 30 years

7. Are you comfortable with the risks?

What if interest rates go up?

As the interest rate is fixed until 31st July 2024, the monthly payment will not change if interest rates go up during the fixed rate period. After the fixed rate ends then both the interest rate and the monthly payment can vary.

The monthly payments shown in this offer could be considerably different if interest rates change. For example, after the fixed rate period ends on 31st July 2024, if the interest rate increases to 10.49% your monthly payment will increase by around £414.50.

RATES MAY INCREASE BY MUCH MORE THAN THIS SO MAKE SURE YOU CAN AFFORD THE MONTHLY PAYMENT.

What if your income goes down?

You will still have to pay your mortgage if you experience a fall in the level of rental income or are unable to let the property out. Think about whether you could do this.

RENTAL INCOME MAY FALL SO MAKE SURE YOU CAN AFFORD THE MONTHLY PAYMENT.

8. What fees must you pay?

Fees payable to The Mortgage Works (UK) plc

	Fee amount
Arrangement Fee (this will be added to the mortgage - not refundable)	£995.00
Funds Transfer Fee (Fee payable for sending the mortgage funds to the conveyancers acting on behalf of The Mortgage Works (UK) plc. This will be deducted from the amount borrowed - not refundable)	£20.00
Mortgage Exit Fee (The current fee payable on full repayment of the mortgage. We will add this to the amount you owe at the time the mortgage is repaid - not refundable)	£90.00

Other Fees

A fee to TIME Mortgage Experts Ltd. for arranging the mortgage (paid when you applied for the mortgage - not refundable)	£595.00

You may have to pay other taxes or costs in addition to any fees shown here.

9. Insurance

Insurance you must take out through The Mortgage Works (UK) plc or TIME Mortgage Experts Ltd

You are not required to buy any insurance through The Mortgage Works (UK) plc or TIME Mortgage Experts Ltd

Insurance you must take out as a condition of this mortgage but that you do not have to take out through The Mortgage Works (UK) plc or TIME Mortgage Experts Ltd

Buildings insurance to cover the full cost of rebuilding the Property

You must arrange insurance to cover your Property before the mortgage starts. If you do not tell us in writing that our insurance is required we will assume that you have arranged your own insurance and that it will commence not later than the date on which the mortgage starts.

Your insurance must comply with the minimum requirements set out in the General Conditions which form part of the Offer

10. What happens if you do not want this mortgage any more?

Early Repayment Charges

Until 31st July 2024, an early repayment charge is payable if you repay the mortgage or vary its terms, for example, by switching to another product. See the table below. A Mortgage exit fee, currently £90.00 is payable if you repay the mortgage at any time.

Cash examples if you repay your mortgage in full

Date of Repayment	Basis of Charge	Amount of Charge
Before 31st July 2020	6%	£5,684.70
1st August 2020 - 31st July 2021	5%	£4,737.25
1st August 2021 - 31st July 2022	4%	£3,789.80
1st August 2022 - 31st July 2023	3%	£2,842.35
1st August 2023 - 31st July 2024	2%	£1,894.90

The early repayment charge will be based on the balance outstanding at the beginning of the month in which the mortgage is repaid

The maximum charge you could pay is £5,684.70, plus a fee which is currently £90.00.

When you repay this mortgage you will only pay interest up to and including the date on which the mortgage is repaid

Please refer to our 'Guide for Mortgages' for further details.

What happens if you move house?

Your mortgage is portable. This means that if you are selling your current property and purchasing a new one at the same time and we are able to offer you a new mortgage, you can transfer the amount you owe on the same terms without having to pay any early repayment charges. If you carry forward less than the amount you owe, any early repayment charge payable will be calculated on the difference. The decision whether or not we will be able to offer you a new mortgage will depend upon the circumstances at the time, including the type of property you want to buy, your personal circumstances and the amount you want to borrow.

The decision whether or not we will be able to offer you a new mortgage will depend upon the circumstances at the time including the type of property you want to buy, your personal circumstances and the amount you want to borrow.

11. What happens if you want to make overpayments?

An overpayment is a payment that is in addition to the minimum payment you must make each month. The minimum payment is shown in Section 6.

You can make a lump sum or regular overpayments of up to £9,474.50, i.e. 10% of the original loan advance amount quoted in Section 6, in each complete 12 month period from the date the mortgage starts until 31st July 2024 without having to pay an early repayment charge unless the whole balance is being repaid in the same month. Amounts above this or where the whole balance is being repaid in the same month are subject to an early repayment charge (as detailed in Section 10).

After 31st July 2024 there are no restrictions on the amounts that you can overpay.

If you make an overpayment the amount you owe us will be reduced immediately and the amount of interest you pay will be reduced from the first day of the following month.

12. Additional features

Incentives

You will receive a cashback of £250.00 when the mortgage starts. This sum will be sent to your conveyancer with the funds for the mortgage loan.

You have chosen a product which includes a free valuation as an incentive. The valuation will only be the basic mortgage valuation carried out on the property for our purposes.
You may want to arrange a more detailed inspection for your own purposes.
You will need to pay for any additional detailed inspection you wish to have carried out at the property.

13. Using a mortgage intermediary

The Mortgage Works (UK) plc will pay TIME Mortgage Experts Ltd and Mortgage Advice Bureau (L&G Club)(GO) £450.00 if you take out this mortgage.

14. Where can you get more information about mortgages?

The Money Advice Service publishes useful guides on choosing a mortgage. These are available free through its website: www.moneyadviceservice.org.uk or by calling 0800 138 7777.

General Information

If you accept this offer, you will not have the right to change your mind and withdraw from the contract after the mortgage starts. However, you can repay the mortgage in full subject to the fees shown in Section 8 and any early repayment charges in Section 10.

All of our mortgages contain a clause which allows us to vary our Managed Variable Rate (Issue 7). If we vary the rate, and at any time part or all of your mortgage is subject to our Managed Variable Rate (Issue 7), we will write and tell you what the new rate is, when it commences and how and when it affects your monthly payments.

This mortgage contract will be concluded in the United Kingdom, in English and will be governed by the law of the country in which the property is located. The Mortgage Works (UK) plc is authorised and regulated by the Financial Conduct Authority and is entered in its register under number 189623.

APPLICANT'S COPY

the mortgage works

REPORT AND VALUATION FOR MORTGAGE

Date of Inspection: 05/06/2019
Reference: 000002

NAME OF APPLICANT

PROPERTY: Vine Street, Hazel Grove, Stockport, Cheshire, SK7 4JP

1. DESCRIPTION: A two storey semi detached dwelling house

Year of construction (approx.) 1990

2. NEW PROPERTIES:
Is builder registered with NHBC/Zurich?

Stage Reached | Is inspection required? no

3. TENURE Freehold | Unexpired Lease Years | Ground Rent £ pa | Maintenance £ pa

4. ACCOMMODATION (Indicate No. of rooms, etc.)

Floors	Reception Rooms	Kitchens(s)	Bedrooms	Bathroom(s)	Internal W.C.s	Other Rooms	Garage/ Space	Outbuildings
2	1	1	2	1	1		Space	0

5. SERVICES (Not Tested)

Electricity	Gas	Main Drainage	Main Water	Central Heating	Hot Water System	Satisfactory Sanitary Arrangements	Is the access satisfactory?
Yes	Yes	Yes	Yes	Gas	Yes	Yes	Yes

6. CONSTRUCTION primary secondary
a) External Walls   Brick
b) Roof   Tile
   Garage   None

7. REPAIRS / ESSENTIAL REPORTS:

Condensation was noted and specialist advice regarding additional heating/ventilation should be obtained and all work implemented. Condensation is a significant health risk.

8. INSURANCE

Full Reinstatement Value £ 99,000   External Floor Area 67 m^2

	Yes / No
(a) Is the property in an area that (to the best of your knowledge) has suffered flooding or is at risk of flooding?	no
(b) Is there any indication of or any reason to anticipate structural damage arising from subsidence, landslip or heave?	no
(c) Are you aware of any subsidence, landslip or heave in the immediate vicinity?	no
(d) Are there any special risks to be considered e.g. the position, exposure, condition of the property or previous losses which could influence an insurer in its acceptance of the property for insurance cover?	no

ie answer to any of these four questions is 'YES' please give full details and recommendations below)

There is evidence that the property has suffered some movement manifested in minor thermal cracking around some window openings. The movement appears longstanding with no evidence of recent or continued movement. A separate report is not considered necessary for mortgage purposes.

9. LEGAL REQUIREMENTS
None.

the mortgage works
common sense lending

REPORT AND VALUATION FOR MORTGAGE

APPLICANT'S COPY
Date of Inspection: 05/06/2019
Reference: 00000

NAME OF APPLICANT	
PROPERTY	Street, Hazel Grove, Stockport, Cheshire, SK7

10. OBSERVATIONS

The property is currently vacant and will be in a condition suitable for letting on the assumption that a) the landlord will comply with all necessary statutory obligations to ensure safe and habitable accommodation and b) all essential works listed in Section 7 will be completed to a satisfactory standard.

The EPC rating for the property is D66 and as such complies with current minimum standards.

Note: This report has been prepared solely for TMW purposes. It is not a structural report and is based upon a limited inspection. It may not reveal serious defects and may contain inaccuracies and omissions. It is unlikely to be adequate for purchasers' purposes and should not be relied upon. You are strongly advised to obtain a fuller report on the property.

11. VALUATION FOR MORTGAGE PURPOSES based on Full vacant possession

(a) In present condition	£125,000	(b) After completion of essential work	£126,000

12. MORTGAGE CLASSIFICATION

If part commercial use, is the residential use   LESS THAN 40%   n/a

13. RENTAL ASSESSMENT

Current Rental Income	£0	Estimated rental income £575	Demand for Letting	Steady

14. CERTIFICATE

The property is suitable security for mortgage purposes

BUYING AT AUCTION AND AUCTION FINANCE

Where I opted not to repeat myself in the last chapter, here I am going to cover somewhat familiar ground. The reason being is that I would like to pair up two topics I've gone into in reasonable detail separately but this time deal with them hand in hand. Any more technical information eg interest rates or different versions / types of auction can be found in MAKING AN OFFER and BRIDGING FINANCE.

Unless you are entirely a cash buyer and even if you are, it is often more prudent to spread these liquid finances around several project than splurge it all on one investment; and you will probably require auction finance. It can be a real gamble trying to purchase via a mortgage at auction. Often mortgage applications take over a month to get to offer stage and this will carry you right past your completion deadline. When that gavel goes down you are on the lock and you have legally exchanged contracts and you will be required there and then to pay 10% of the purchase price plus admin fees as a deposit on the property. You will most likely be given a 28 day deadline to complete and if you haven't done so then you leave yourself open to legal repercussions eg losing your deposit and other reparation costs. In fact that 28 day stopwatch doesn't actually start until your solicitor has received a copy of the draft contract, which will be accompanied by the auction pack. The auction pack is basically all the legal work that both solicitors would usually do separately but because of the brevity necessary for the transaction, it has already been completed by the vendors solicitor eg he will do the necessary searches so there is no need to wait weeks for their arrival and their potential to be adverse. The auction pack is also available for you to peruse before you start bidding. This way you can see any problems that may hinder or dissuade you from making an offer; these problems can often be reasons why a mortgage company wouldn't lend on the property. You will then be certain that you need to secure another means of finance. You will often also be required to pay some or all of the vendors costs in these matters so look out for that when looking through the information.

Considering your timescale it is probably safer to apply for auction finance. You can approach a lender before the auction to secure an agreement in principle; a very sensible approach. There should also be enough time to secure the finance within the deadline, after the hammer has dropped. The finance will rest upon roughly the same criterion that your mortgage lender may require but they may be more lenient when it comes to your proof of income and they may take capital gains profit into account. They tend to do desk top valuations at the lower end of the market (below £500,000) rather than sending a surveyor out which, saves a good 2 weeks in the process. The LTV you will be required to put down will most likely be 75% and your interest rates will be a lot higher than a mortgage company would charge, because it is a short term loan. It may be worth considering applying for both (but ask your FA). If the mortgage doesn't come through then use the bridge.

So now you've been browsing the auction catalogues and watching Homes Under The Hammer; you are good to go! You've seen a house or two that have taken your fancy and on first look, there is some profit to be made.

Side note: I'm not going to talk to you about buying commercial property, new home building or buying land because I am a lot less informed on those than BTLs and house renovation, although I have done a fair amount of homework ready for my first leap.

Now, like 'Homes Under The Hammer' constantly remind you: check out the property information pack (for reasons I imparted to you previously). You don't want to buy a flat and realise there are humongous maintenance fees or a house with only 50 years left on the leasehold. If you are inexperienced then take a copy to a solicitor to scan through. A little money at the start could save you thousands at the end; literally!

When you arrange a viewing you will no doubt be a part of a block viewing, as an auction property generally drums up a lot of interest, which is the point! Don't let the crowds put you off your game and don't forget your renovation check list. You don't need some awful case of subsidence passing you by. Again if you can get an expert to accompany you, all the better.

Side note: I viewed a property one day which looked like a real bargain and was close to where I lived. I poked my head excitedly down into the cellar only to find where they kept the swimming pool. There was a pump doing its damnedest to expel the water and it wasn't evident if there had just been a flood or there was a water table issue or what. The first thing I wanted to know was whether the house was subsiding as a result. The agent won't tell you this as they are not qualified. They won't let you in on any other surveys that might have been done because they would have to have the express permission of the ex buyer who commissioned it or the vendor if they had. Plus they want to sell the house so they want to keep that kind of news under wraps until you are financially more committed. Any way the floor looked to be on a slope and I wondered if the room was sinking. It struck me that if this was poor original building then the number of bricks at the lower end would be more than in the course at the higher end ie it is just a sloppy floor. If it's the same then the house is moving. Spoiler, the house was moving! This was confirmed to me by a mate doing a drive way a year later for the new owners and apparently the whole affair had been an expensive nightmare; all due to the position of an historic pond. A little nimble thinking can save you a lot of time and effort!

As mentioned earlier in the book, a vendor is often willing to sell their property before the auction for the right price. In fact the catalogue often says specifically if they are not. The reserve is the undisclosed fee that the vendor is willing to part with the property for and is usually around 10% above or below the guide price. This figure must be reached before the property can be sold and as previously mentioned the sale is legally binding on the fall of the hammer. You now have 28 days from receipt of a draft contract to complete the sale.

When you arrive at the auction you will have to supply some personal information including Photo ID and proof of address. You will be registered and then duly directed to the auction room. The room should be full of people waiting to bid on their chosen property(s) and the auctioneer will proceed in order through the catalogue property by property accepting bids and trying to drum up the best price for the vendors. I will give you first hand a description of this in one of the case studies.

EDWARD mellor auction

MEM

Auction Date: _____

Property Address:

Lot 50
Stockport Road East
Bredbury
Stockport
SK6

Vendor's Solicitor:

Thompson & Cooke
12 Stamford Street
Stalybridge
SK15 1LA

```
*** CUSTOMER COPY ***
EDWARD MELLOR LIMITED
STOCKPORT
WWW.EDWARDMELLOR.CO.U
Thank you

14:34:47        17/07/18
                Receipt 0280
AID ....05084       IIC ....2635
VISA DEBIT
************
A0000000031010           CHIP
SALE            £9,496.00

   PIN VERIFIED
    APPROVED
    AUTH CODE: 00771
2793012427A1558
5:2
   PLEASE DEBIT MY ACCOUNT
   WITH THE TOTAL AMOUNT
PLEASE RETAIN RECEIPT
```

I/We _____
hereby acknowledge myself/ourselves to be the Purchaser(s) of the above Lot, described in the foregoing Particulars at the sum of:

_____ (£ 85,000)

and I/We have paid the sum of:

_____ (£ 9,500)

to Edward Mellor Ltd as a deposit and in part payment of the purchase money. I/We agree to pay the remainder thereof and to complete the purchase in accordance with the annexed Particulars and Conditions of Sale in all respects. Completion is to take place 28 days from the date below unless otherwise specified in the Special Conditions. I have read and understand any Special Conditions and Amendments.

DATED this _____ day of _____ 20 18

Purchase Price: £ 85,000
Less 10% deposit: £ 9,500
(Minimum £3000)

Balance: £ 76,500

SIGNED BY THE PURCHASER: ✗ _____

Signed as Agents for the Vendor: _____
We ratify the Sale and acknowledge receipt of the above-mentioned Deposit in accordance with the Conditions of Sale.

PURCHASER'S SOLICITORS

Full Name: _____
Address: SAS Daniels
30 Great Street
Stockport
                        SK3
Postcode: _____
Telephone: 0161 475 7680

PURCHASER'S DETAILS

Full Name: _____
Address: _____
          Hazel Grove
          Stockport
                        SK7
Postcode: _____
Telephone: _____

PRICE RENEGOTIATION AFTER SURVEY

Whether you are purchasing residentially (a much more common occurrence) or in our case BTL, when your survey comes back it may say the property is in good condition and values up (the value is the same as the price that you are paying for it). In this case you are free to carry on with the legal side and progress through your purchase. As previously mentioned, you need to have finalised any negotiations as a result of this survey before moving on to the legal side. There are a myriad combinations of issues that can arrive as a result of an adverse survey but here are a few common problems:

THE VALUER DOWN VALUES THE PROPERTY

For example, you offered the asking price but the valuation has come back £10,000 less. This means that the lender will only lend you the LTV of this new value. You will then have to: get the vendor to agree a reduction because the property isn't worth as much as you offered; make up the difference with your own cash; do a mixture of both; or you could pull out of the sale altogether. This situation is not black and white, it is a grey scale, so you sometimes need to be a little creative and the estate agent can be a great guide.

You can also appeal the decision, which requires you doing so formally, accompanied by your evidence, which needs to consist of 3 examples of completed comparable properties. I have tried this course of action on more than one occasion and it has always been a waste of time. The ridiculous fact about the process is that the judge and jury of this kangaroo court is the surveyor who did the original valuation. I expect he/she is not in a rush to admit he's crap at his/her job.

THE SURVEYOR DOWN VALUES THE RENTAL VALUATION

If the property is in need of renovation then this is a common issue and it means that the lender's rental calculation will not fit the criterion. In each instance I have experienced, the lender will up the deposit requirement (lower the LTV). If you haven't got much of a slush fund then this can be a deal breaker.

THE SURVEYOR FLAGS UP REPAIRS THAT HE CONSIDERS ESSENTIAL TO LENDING

Depending on the lender, they may still carry on and lend anyway at the original price but a lender can down value the property in its current condition and usually by an estimate of what the surveyor considers the reparation works to cost eg

£195,000 in current condition
£200,000 when works completed
£5,000 retention

Here they estimate that the building work will cost no more than £5,000. First they will ask for relevant contractors to enter the property and write a report including a quote. They will then amend the retention accordingly. They will hold the money back until the work is done between exchange and completion (usually) or within a certain time frame after completion and release the full amount of funds at the point the works are finished.

Now this is more likely to happen on a residential sale and to be fair it is a little outmoded. In my experience, in recent times, the lender (certainly on BTLs) is more likely to just lend you the lower figure and let you do the work in your own sweet time, forgoing the reports altogether (unless perhaps there are serious structural suspicions).

BTL lending is usually less stringent when it comes to this part of the application because you are considered to know what you are doing, as this is an investment and also you are putting down a larger deposit than with a typical residential application.

Side note: if you are a first time renovator, it may be worth your while getting a more in-depth survey. What is known as a 'homebuyers' report can be procured privately (and via the lender for residential mortgages). I say this because I've never been offered the option on a BTL. This will go into greater depth and discuss everything in the property. The surveyor will go into great detail about all aspects of the property (incidentally they are not structural engineers) and grade their findings as to the urgency of any findings they consider noteworthy: this is usually based on a number or traffic light system. The reports are around the £400 / £500 mark. Do beware though not to let this report scare the living daylights out of you, especially if you are a novice. As an estate agent

I've seen a lot of these and a lot of buyers pull out of purchases unnecessarily because they have taken every advisory point as something that needs urgent attention or is about to fail. The surveyor needs to earn his money, so he will leave no stone unturned or uncommented on in order to cover his back the best he can. You should take heed of the items he has flagged up as 'red' and take the rest under advisement.

COMPLETION DAY AND ONWARDS

First I'm going to talk about renovation. Feel free to skip this part if you have bought a property ready to move in to and go to the start of THE FINISHED HOUSE.

It's completion day and sometime more often than not after 1pm (ie solicitors lunch time) you will get a call to say that the vendor's solicitor has received the money and the house is now yours. It's time to get to work as fast as possible because in this instance time really is money. You are paying a mortgage and probably council tax out every month and a little bit on utilities too. That reminds me that, although you won't be using a lot of gas, electric and water, you will be using some and you will need to pay for it; utility companies are touchy about that. Plus you want your profit <u>ASAP</u>! Obviously you need to choose the best deal and you can use compare portals for that, but because you won't be using too much you want to see what the cheapest standing charges are - the daily rate you are charged regardless of your usage. Set up a direct debit to the gas or electric company for £10 per month each and that should cover you. Water rates are going to rely on which company runs your area; call them for a quote. Just for clarity, your plasterer will need a water supply for mixing and so will any builders. Also people like to wash their hands, go to the toilet (not necessarily in that order) and make a brew amongst other things. Gas will be needed for central heating in winter for your contractors and also for drying out plaster and paint. Electricity will be needed for power tools, lighting and to ignite the combi boiler; oh and most importantly, that kettle.

There is certainly an order in which you want to approach the works - you wouldn't put new flooring down and then get stuck into the damp course would you? So here is a logical order to follow:

1) Hire a builder's skip
2) Remove anything you don't want or need from the property eg wallpaper, loose plaster, tatty woodwork (skirting board, architrave etc), old pipes, bad wiring and of course the out of date kitchen and bathroom. This certainly isn't an exhaustive list.
3) Complete any structural work that needs doing and start any extension work. I'm not going to delve into the planning and regulations involved, it is beyond the scope of this book and included only for comprehensiveness
4) Repair any roof defects if they are causing water to enter the property. If it is a simple overhaul, then it can be completed concurrently with other works
5) Pointing, again unless it is causing no internal problems, then this can also be done in the background too
6) Knock down or create any walls you require internally
7) (Assuming you have completed any extension) start installing windows and external doors
8) Gas first fix, as this is most likely to need some under floor board installation. Gas pipes may also need to traverse floors and scale walls. Gas pipes

will start at the gas meter and spread out from there
9) Most plumbing will also have the same requirements. Soil pipes that need re-routing can also cause some upheaval. All the water pipes will emanate from the pipe where the stop tap is
10) First fix for the electrics. The electrical wires span out from the electric meter via the consumer unit to the rest of the house. Although the wiring will also spread through the whole property, most electrical wires will be installed and travel through chased out channels in the plaster of the walls. The cavities for the sockets and light switches will also need chasing out
11) Plastering, plasterboard, and skimming the walls and ceiling. The property will really start to look closer to the finished product now
12) Joinery. This is when you need to add your architrave, internal doors, bannisters and skirting boards
13) Fit the kitchen
14) Fit the bathroom
15) Paint walls and the woodwork
16) Carpet and flooring installation
17) Landscape the outside. This can also be done adjacent to other works

Land Registry

Official copy of register of title

Title number GM **Edition date 14.02.2017**

- This official copy shows the entries on the register of title on 20 Feb 2017 at 10:50:03.
- This date must be quoted as the "search from date" in any official search application based on this copy.
- The date at the beginning of an entry is the date on which the entry was made in the register.
- Issued on 20 Feb 2017.
- Under s.67 of the Land Registration Act 2002, this copy is admissible in evidence to the same extent as the original.
- This title is dealt with by Land Registry Fylde Office.

A: Property Register

This register describes the land and estate comprised in the title.

GREATER MANCHESTER : TAMESIDE

1. (03.06.1977) The Freehold land shown edged with red on the plan of the above Title filed at the Registry and being Wood, Hollingworth, Hyde (SK14).

2. The land has the benefit of the rights granted by the Conveyance dated 1 March 1787 referred to in the Charges Register.

3. The land has the benefit of the rights granted by but is subject to the rights reserved by the Conveyance dated 7 April 1977 referred to in the Charges Register.

4. The Conveyance dated 7 April 1977 referred to in the Charges Register contains a provision as to light or air.

B: Proprietorship Register

This register specifies the class of title and identifies the owner. It contains any entries that affect the right of disposal.

Title absolute

1. (04.01.1985) PROPRIETOR: WILLIAM MICHAEL of Wood, Hollingworth, Hyde SK14

2. The Transfer to the proprietor contains a covenant to observe and perform the covenants referred to in the Charges Register and of indemnity in respect thereof.

3. (14.02.2017) RESTRICTION: No disposition of the registered estate by the proprietor of the registered estate is to be registered without a written consent signed by PXS 3 Limited Co. Regn. No. 03912950 of 1 New Change, London EX4M 9AF or by their conveyancer.

C: Charges Register

This register contains any charges and other matters that affect the land.

Title number GM

1. The land in this title is with other land subject to a perpetual yearly rentcharge of £3.16.6d created by a Conveyance dated 1 March 1787 made between (1) William   and (2) Daniel

   NOTE: Copy filed.

2. By a Conveyance dated 7 April 1977 made between (1) Frank Sylvester   and (2) David Francis   this rentcharge was informally apportioned as to £3.07 to the land in this title.

   NOTE: Copy filed.

3. The Conveyance dated 1 March 1787 referred to above contains covenants.

4. The Conveyance dated 7 April 1977 referred to above contains restrictive covenants.

End of register

H.M. LAND REGISTRY	TITLE NUMBER		
	GM		
ORDNANCE SURVEY PLAN REFERENCE	SK	SECTION E	Scale 1/1250
COUNTY GREATER MANCHESTER DISTRICT TAMESIDE			© Crown copyright 1976

Law Society Property Information Form (3rd edition)

Address of the property

STREET
HAZEL GROVE

Postcode: S K 7 _ 4 _ _

Full names of the seller

MISS J

Seller's solicitor

Name of solicitor's firm: JONES LAW PARTNERSHIP

Address:
VERNON CHAMBERS
11 MARKET STREET
MARPLE
SK6 7AA

Email: @joneslawpartnership.co.uk

Reference number: V / L

About this form

This form is completed by the seller to supply the detailed information and documents which may be relied upon for the conveyancing process.

Definitions

It is important that sellers and buyers read the notes below.

- 'Seller' means all sellers together where the property is owned by more than one person.
- 'Buyer' means all buyers together where the property is being bought by more than one person.
- 'Property' includes all buildings and land within its boundaries.

Boundaries

If the property is leasehold this section, or parts of it, may not apply.

1.1 Looking towards the property from the road, who owns or accepts responsibility to maintain or repair the boundary features:

(a) on the left? ☐ Seller ☐ Neighbour ☑ Shared ☐ Not known

(b) on the right? ☐ Seller ☐ Neighbour ☑ Shared ☐ Not known

(c) at the rear? ☐ Seller ☐ Neighbour ☑ Shared ☐ Not known

(d) at the front? ☑ Seller ☐ Neighbour ☐ Shared ☐ Not known

1.2 If the boundaries are irregular please indicate ownership by written description or by reference to a plan:

N/A.

1.3 Is the seller aware of any boundary feature having been moved in the last 20 years? If Yes, please give details: ☐ Yes ☑ No

1.4 During the seller's ownership, has any land previously forming part of the property been sold or has any adjacent property been purchased? If Yes, please give details: ☐ Yes ☑ No

1.5 Does any part of the property or any building on the property overhang, or project under, the boundary of the neighbouring property or road? If Yes, please give details: ☐ Yes ☑ No

Law Society Fittings and Contents Form (3rd edition)

Address of the property

GRUNDEY STREET
HAZEL GROVE

Postcode: S K 7 _ _ _ _

Full names of the seller

Seller's solicitor

Name of solicitor's firm

JONES LAW PARTNERSHIP

Address

VERNON CHAMBERS
11 MARKET STREET
MARPLE
SK1 7AA

Email

@joneslawpartnership.co.uk

Reference number

About this form

The aim of this form is to make clear to the buyer which items are included in the sale. It must be completed accurately by the seller as the form may become part of the contract between the buyer and seller.

It is important that sellers and buyers check the information in this form carefully.

Definitions

- 'Seller' means all sellers together where the property is owned by more than one person.
- 'Buyer' means all buyers together where the property is being bought by more than one person.

Instructions to the seller and the buyer

In each row, the seller should tick the appropriate box to show whether:

- the item is included in the sale ('*Included*');
- the item is excluded from the sale ('*Excluded*');
- there is no such item at the property ('*None*').

Where an item is excluded from the sale the seller may offer it for sale by inserting a price in the appropriate box. The buyer can then decide whether to accept the seller's offer.

A seller who inserts a price in this form is responsible for negotiating the sale of that item directly with the buyer or through their estate agent. If the seller or buyer instructs their solicitor to negotiate the sale of such an item, there may be an additional charge.

Sellers and buyers should inform their solicitors of any arrangements made about items offered for sale.

If the seller removes any fixtures, fittings or contents, the seller should be reasonably careful to ensure that any damage caused is minimised.

Unless stated otherwise, the seller will be responsible for ensuring that all rubbish is removed from the property (including from the loft, garden, outbuildings, garages and sheds), and that the property is left in a reasonably clean and tidy condition.

Basic fittings

	Included	Excluded	None	Price	Comments
Boiler/immersion heater	✓				
Radiators/wall heaters	✓				
Night-storage heaters			✓		
Free-standing heaters			✓		
Gas fires (with surround)	✓				
Electric fires (with surround)	✓				
Light switches	✓				
Roof insulation	✓				
Window fittings	✓				
Window shutters/grilles			✓		
Internal door fittings	✓				
External door fittings	✓				
Doorbell/chime	✓				

This Underlease

is made the tenth day of January One thousand nine hundred and thirty Between Robert Chadwick formerly of 61 King George Road Hyde in the County of Chester but now of 180 Mottram Old Road Hyde aforesaid Agent (hereinafter called "the Lessor") of the one part and Ethel Jean Cumberlidge the wife of Thomas Henry Cumberlidge of The Tohlaw Wood End Lane Hyde aforesaid Provision Merchant (hereinafter called "the Lessee") of the other part Whereas:

1. By an Underlease (hereinafter referred to as "the Underlease") dated the twenty fourth day of March One thousand nine hundred and ten and made between Joseph Thornycroft of the first part John Harper Brompton of the second part and James Bewley of the third part All that plot of land situate in Stockport Road Bredbury in the said County of Chester containing four hundred and eleven square yards or thereabouts bounded on the northerly side thereof by and including one half in width of a passage nine feet wide on the northeasterly side by land belonging to the Great Central Railway Company on the westerly side thereof by land and premises sold to Charlotte Anne Chadwick and on the southerly side by Stockport Road leading from Stockport to Woodley and which plot of land was more particularly delineated and

Energy Performance Certificate

HM Government

Hollingworth, HYDE, SK14

Dwelling type:	Mid-terrace house
Date of assessment:	19 December 2016
Date of certificate:	19 December 2016
Reference number:	9918-2984-7282-4186-7984
Type of assessment:	RdSAP, existing dwelling
Total floor area:	100 m²

Use this document to:
- Compare current ratings of properties to see which properties are more energy efficient
- Find out how you can save energy and money by installing improvement measures

Estimated energy costs of dwelling for 3 years:	£ 4,992
Over 3 years you could save	£ 2,646

Estimated energy costs of this home

	Current costs	Potential costs	Potential future savings
Lighting	£ 210 over 3 years	£ 210 over 3 years	
Heating	£ 3,573 over 3 years	£ 1,821 over 3 years	You could save £ 2,646 over 3 years
Hot Water	£ 1,209 over 3 years	£ 315 over 3 years	
Totals	£ 4,992	£ 2,346	

These figures show how much the average household would spend in this property for heating, lighting and hot water and is not based on energy used by individual households. This excludes energy use for running appliances like TVs, computers and cookers, and electricity generated by microgeneration.

Energy Efficiency Rating

Current: 46
Potential: 84

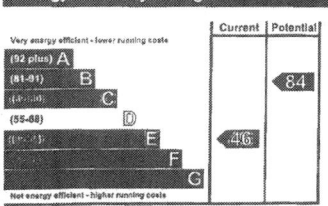

The graph shows the current energy efficiency of your home.

The higher the rating the lower your fuel bills are likely to be.

The potential rating shows the effect of undertaking the recommendations on page 3.

The average energy efficiency rating for a dwelling in England and Wales is band D (rating 60).

The EPC rating shown here is based on standard assumptions about occupancy and energy use and may not reflect how energy is consumed by individual occupants.

Top actions you can take to save money and make your home more efficient

Recommended measures	Indicative cost	Typical savings over 3 years	Available with Green Deal
1 Increase loft insulation to 270 mm	£100 - £350	£ 258	✓
2 Internal or external wall insulation	£4,000 - £14,000	£ 1,161	✓
3 Floor insulation (solid floor)	£4,000 - £6,000	£ 90	✓

See page 3 for a full list of recommendations for this property.

To find out more about the recommended measures and other actions you could take today to save money, visit www.gov.uk/energy-grants-calculator or call 0300 123 1234 (standard national rate). The Green Deal may enable you to make your home warmer and cheaper to run.

Hollingworth, HYDE, SK14
19 December 2016   RRN: 9618-2984-7262-4166-7964

Energy Performance Certificate

Summary of this home's energy performance related features

Element	Description	Energy Efficiency
Walls	Sandstone or limestone, as built, no insulation (assumed)	★☆☆☆☆
Roof	Pitched, 50 mm loft insulation	★★☆☆☆
Floor	Solid, no insulation (assumed)	—
Windows	Fully double glazed	★★★☆☆
Main heating	Electric storage heaters	★★★☆☆
Main heating controls	Controls for high heat retention storage heaters	★★★★☆
Secondary heating	Room heaters, electric	—
Hot water	Electric immersion, off-peak	★☆☆☆☆
Lighting	Low energy lighting in all fixed outlets	★★★★★

Current primary energy use per square metre of floor area: 524 kWh/m² per year

The assessment does not take into consideration the physical condition of any element. 'Assumed' means that the insulation could not be inspected and an assumption has been made in the methodology based on age and type of construction.

Low and zero carbon energy sources

Low and zero carbon energy sources are sources of energy that release either very little or no carbon dioxide into the atmosphere when they are used. Installing these sources may help reduce energy bills as well as cutting carbon. There are none provided for this home.

Your home's heat demand

For most homes, the vast majority of energy costs derive from heating the home. Where applicable, this table shows the energy that could be saved in this property by insulating the loft and walls, based on typical energy use (shown within brackets as it is a reduction in energy use).

Heat demand	Existing dwelling	Impact of loft insulation	Impact of cavity wall insulation	Impact of solid wall insulation
Space heating (kWh per year)	13,725	(996)	N/A	(4,492)
Water heating (kWh per year)	2,922			

You could receive Renewable Heat Incentive (RHI) payments and help reduce carbon emissions by replacing your existing heating system with one that generates renewable heat, subject to meeting minimum energy efficiency requirements. The estimated energy required for space and water heating will form the basis of the payments. For more information, search for the domestic RHI on the www.gov.uk website.

Environmental Risk Management
RPS
Provided by

Homecheck

Professional Opinion
Environmental Risk

Certificate

This Certificate is issued in respect of the Homecheck Professional Environmental Report 48305566_1 dated 12/08/2013 for the property described as:

GREEN ROAD
DENTON
MANCHESTER
M34

Your Reference: ATD-1260773-RWV7_HCP

Contaminated Land Assessment

RPS certifies that the level of environmental risk identified in the Homecheck Professional Environmental Report is not likely to be sufficient for the property to be described as "contaminated land" as defined by section 78(A)2 of Part 2A of the Environmental Protection Act 1990.

Lending Assessment

As the subject property has received a Certificate, it is the opinion of RPS that "contaminated land" issues should not have a significant impact on the security of the property for normal lending purposes.

Landfill Site: The report highlights landfill within 500m of the property. A study published by the Department for Environment Food and Rural Affairs on 21 February 2003 indicates a possible impact on value of UK properties which are located near landfill sites. It is recommended that you contact your surveyor and ascertain if the location of the landfill has impact on the value in this instance.

Completed by:
RPS Environmental Risk Team

RPS

Dated 12 August 2013

This Certificate is based only on the information relating to historical land uses as shown by data sources collated by Sitescope Ltd and stated within the Homecheck Professional Environmental Report. This Certificate should be read in conjunction with both that Report and the Guide to the RPS Environmental Risk Certificate provided with this Certificate. No physical inspection of the Property has been carried out. This Certificate is subject to our prevailing terms of business as set out in the document entitled Sitescope Terms and Conditions.

Other Matters

Whilst outside the scope of Part 2A of the Environmental Protection Act 1990, and this Certificate, it should also be noted that the following additional environmental factors have been identified within the Report:

Coal Mining: The property is in or near a coal mining area. A coal mining search may be required. (See Section C.1)

Order: 48305566_1   hcp_risk_letter v36.0

The COAL AUTHORITY

Issued by
The Coal Authority, Property Search Services, 200 Lichfield Lane, Berry Hill, Mansfield, Nottinghamshire, NG18 4RG
Website: www.groundstability.com   Phone: 0845 762 6848   DX 716176 MANSFIELD 5

ETSOS	Our reference:	51000356853001
WILLOW MILL	Your reference:	ATD-1273949-MEBE
UNIT 2-5 FELL VIEW	Date of your enquiry:	28 August 2013
CATON	Date we received your enquiry:	28 August 2013
LANCASTER	Date of issue:	28 August 2013
LANCASHIRE		
LA2 9RA		

This report is for the property described in the address below and the attached plan.

Residential Coal Authority Mining Report

GREEN ROAD, DENTON, MANCHESTER, M34 7

This report is based on and limited to the records held by, the Coal Authority, and the Cheshire Brine Subsidence Compensation Board's records, at the time we answer the search.

Coal mining	See comments below
Brine Compensation District	No

Information from the Coal Authority

Underground coal mining

Past

The property is in the likely zone of influence from workings in 2 seams of coal at 100m to 300m depth, and last worked in 1882.

Any ground movement from these coal workings should have stopped by now.

Present

The property is not in the likely zone of influence of any present underground coal workings.

Future

The property is not in an area for which the Coal Authority is determining whether to grant a licence to remove coal using underground methods.

The property is not in an area for which a licence has been granted to remove or otherwise work coal using underground methods.

The property is not in an area that is likely to be affected at the surface from any planned future workings.

However, reserves of coal exist in the local area which could be worked at some time in the future.

No notice of the risk of the land being affected by subsidence has been given under section 46 of the Coal Mining Subsidence Act 1991.

Mine entries

Within, or within 20 metres of, the boundary of the property there is 1 mine entry, the approximate position of which is shown on the attached plan.

CON29DW
DRAINAGE AND WATER ENQUIRY

United Utilities

Drainage and Water Enquiry
The information in this document refers to: -

Property: **GREEN ROAD DENTON MANCHESTER M34**

This document was produced by: -

ETSOS
Units 2-5 Willow Mill
Fell View
Caton
Lancaster
LA2 9RA

Client Ref: ATD-1260771-FQJU

FAO:

United Utilities Water PLC
Property Searches
Ground Floor Grasmere House
Lingley Mere Business Park
Great Sankey
Warrington
WA5 3LP

Telephone 0870 7510101

Facsimile 0870 7510102

e-mail - property.searches@uuplc.co.uk

DX 715568 Warrington 7

The following records were searched in compiling this report:-
The Map of Public Sewers, the Map of Waterworks, Water and Sewerage billing records, Adoption of Public Sewer records, Building Over Public Sewer records, the Register of Properties subject to Internal Foul Flooding, Adoption of Public Water Mains records, the Register of Properties subject to Poor Water Pressure and the Drinking Water Register. All of these are held by United Utilities Water PLC, Haweswater House, Lingley Mere Business Park, Lingley Green Avenue, Great Sankey, Warrington, WA5 3LP.

United Utilities Water PLC is liable in respect of the following: -

(i) any negligent or incorrect entry in the records searched;

(ii) any negligent or incorrect interpretation of the records searched; and

(iii) any negligent or incorrect recording of that interpretation in the search report

(iv) compensation payments

United Utilities Water PLC
Registered in England & Wales No. 2366678
Registered Office Haweswater House, Lingley Mere

Entry Date 12/08/2013 Response Date 15/08/2013   UU Ref: 957851

SEARCH & TITLE REPORT

Search Report

Local Search – see attached

(Please note, this search will only reveal planning entries specific to the property you are purchasing. To check whether any neighbouring properties have planning applications, please contact your local authority).

This has revealed the following:-

1. The road fronting the property is adopted by the council and therefore maintained at public expense.

2. The property is located within a "smoke control area". Under the Clean Air Act local authorities may declare the whole or part of the district of the authority to be a smoke control area. It is an offence to emit smoke from a chimney of a building, from a furnace or from any fixed boiler if located in a designated smoke control area. It is also an offence to acquire an "unauthorised fuel" for use within a smoke control area unless it is used in an "exempt" appliance ("exempted" from the controls which generally apply in the smoke control area). The current maximum level of fine is £1,000 for each offence.

Environmental Search – see attached

Enclosed is a copy of the Environmental Report. You will see from the certificate that the property is not at risk from having been built on contaminated land.

The search has revealed the property is in an area which may be affected by **Coal Mining** activity. We will undertake the coal mining search for you at a cost of £49.20.

The search has revealed **potential flooding** in the area of the property. This may have an impact on the value and resale ability. Please check with your property insurer and confirm back to me that you are able to insure the property on satisfactory terms.

For your protection, and the protection of your lender, we have undertaken a flood report. This examines whether the property maybe situated on or near land which could be susceptible to flooding. The purpose of this is to identify from available data whether there are current and potential flood risks which could result in your property being flooded or adversely affect your ability to obtain suitable insurance cover. The report will cost £24 inc VAT.

Please note this environmental report does not provide detailed information as to whether the property is affected by fracking, nuclear installation or power stations, solar/wind farms or the proposed HS2 rail route. If you would like further information on any of these items, please contact the office and we can order a further energy report at a further cost, otherwise we advise you to seek further information as to the location of the sights and whether they will affect the property in any way.

THE FINISHED HOUSE

Hopefully you are no further on than 3 months after completion, the work has been carried out to your satisfaction and all your certificates are in; including your gas safety and electrical certificate. It's finally time to get the estate agent back in to do a valuation of the property and see what you have achieved (potentially) in increased value and also what you are expecting in the way of a monthly rental figure (monthly income potential).

Also you need to be mindful that if you have taken out a bridging loan or are solely planning on remortgaging the property to release equity, you are a month away from speaking to your FA again; put a reminder in your diary for this in capital letters.

If all has gone to plan this should be the real cherry on the cake and vindication for all your savvy and hard work. But don't let off your party popper yet, you've still got to secure a tenant.

I would advise you get at least 3 agents in, including the agent you originally bought the property from. The more advice and opinions you can get, the more able you will be to make an informed decision and go with the right agent (especially when this advice is free). Hopefully their figures will be in the same ball park. Some agents (and one nation wide company comes straight to my mind) will deliberately over value so as to get you on the market. For them if they sell or rent at this overinflated figure then they are the hero and if not, then they can just tell you that it's the market's fault and selling a property is a trial and error process (or something of that ilk); you need to reduce the price. This is fine if you secure a rent or sale at this higher price but I would bet in the majority of cases that you just waste a month of marketing time as well as a mortgage and council tax payment. If that turns into two months then you are on the way to losing the extra you thought you were going to get. Plus your property may sit on Rightmove going stale. Also remember that there could be a big difference in the agents' fees. Like with solicitors, the cheapest one isn't always the right choice. Check reviews on Google and word of mouth. It may be worth doing a board count around the area (drive around or check Rightmove) as this will give you an idea of who the daddy is in your area.

Let's say the valuations were all roughly the same and so was the sales patter. You chose the agent you bought the property through, as it's good form and you will reap the benefits if you offer on a property with them again in the future.

High street estate agents are usually no sale / rent, no fee. So after serving their (eg 30 day) notice you can change agents if you are not happy with the results of their marketing. Or you could go joint / multi agency ie having a two or more agents marketing the property. For me this looks desperate and can put people off or invite much lower offers if you are selling. It is likely to cost a little more as the agent's fees will be split into winner / loser proportions. Plus they have to agree to it as well.

You could also try a web based agent who will be cheaper and you will get your spot on Rightmove and a for sale board, which is all you really need to find a buyer / renter but you will pay up front and if you are not happy with their results then you either have to sit there sucking your lemon or lose the cash and go elsewhere and pay the next guy his commission too.

How long you should give an agent is up to you. If a month has gone by and you aren't getting any offers, or worse still, any viewers, then something needs to change. It might not necessarily be the agent, it could be the price or there may be something about the property eg style, photos or footprint putting people off. You need to have a frank conversation with your agent, maybe you haven't listened to their advise in the first place. Any property in any area will sell at the right price! It's whether you can or are willing to let it go at that.

If you have decided to sell the property the earliest you can do this is 6 months after completion due to money laundering rules. You can sell as soon as you want with a bridging loan or a cash purchase but if your buyer is purchasing using a mortgage, they will not be allowed to buy the house unless you have owned it for 6 months. So with a bridge or cash you can complete a sale on the 6 month half anniversary of your purchase but remember it is a condition of your BTL mortgage that you are required to let the property out at least for one 6 month short hold assured tenancy. So your sale would have to complete on the last day of the tenancy. In either case this doesn't mean you can't market the property as soon as it is ready to show but consider your tenants feelings as they will be subjected to the possibility of many people tramping through their home until you find a buyer.

If you are selling the property, hopefully you will be satisfied with the solicitor who dealt with the purchase of your property and therefore the sensible course of action would be to retain their services again for the sale. The selling solicitors fees should be cheaper than those of the buying fees because there are less disbursements to pay for. You will need to provide photo ID again, proof of address, and fill in the fixtures and fittings list (what is included in the sale of the property) and a property information form.

At the end of the sale don't forget that you will need to consider the implications of capital gains tax and income tax if you have made any rental profit. See an expert for advice!

In case you have skipped through any of the book and you are wondering why I have only covered selling your renovation and nothing on finding a tenant; please look back to the chapter on tenancy agreements.

REMORTGAGES AND FURTHER ADVANCES

When I would hear of someone remortgaging their house, my mind used to jump to the conclusion that they'd run up a load of debt: it never sounded like a positive move.

Cut to the present day and I've remortgaged so many houses so many times. In reality remortgaging just means that you are changing the product that you have funded the property purchase with.

Let's say you bought a house to rent at a 2 year fixed rate. It's a few months prior to the end of the term and the mortgage lender has sent you a letter saying as such, and that you will be placed on their variable rate in two months. This rate will be substantially higher than the rate you were previously on and affect your rental profit significantly. It's time to see your FA.

Just as before when you originally chose your mortgage, you will set about choosing a new product. Obviously this will require the same process as last time although your valuation fee is likely to be less; they will still send a surveyor out to your property though. In fact you are often able to continue on the same or similar product with the same lender. You will be able to avoid paying a valuation fee altogether in this case with some lenders. Your FA may also charge you less as there is less work involved in a remortgage application than with a purchase.

If you are lucky enough, then your property may have increased in value due to a favourable market during your fixed period and you may even be able to release some equity. The mortgage company will often want to know what that money is to be spent on. They will generally want to hear that it's for another property purchase or property renovation; not a holiday in the Bahamas! If you opt to take out some equity you will obviously be paying more on your mortgage payments and will be making less monthly profit from your investment. You may not be taking a lot out but even if you are, you could still be benefiting from a more favourable interest rate. I have remortgaged property to release equity and ended up paying less than I was previously in monthly payments. This is generally dependent on the economy at the time!

Let's say the property you have bought needs renovating. You bought the property knowing that there was a profit or at least some equity to be made out of doing it up and renting it out. Now you don't need to wait for the full term of your fixed rate to expire. In fact you can sell the property anytime you want to as long as you have owned it for 6 months. This is due to money laundering stipulations. Also the mortgage company requires at least one 6 month short hold assured tenancy to have been completed before sale (no 3 month lets). So this timescale adds up to the renovation time + marketing time + rental period. Obviously if you are buying a property in rentable condition then you forgo the renovation time. By selling the property in the fixed period, you will, as previously discussed, incur a penalty. This is something you have to budget for before buying the property, so you can accurately gauge any equity / profit you will gain in the future.

Some lenders will let you do a further advance. It's like a remortgage but you stay on the same product with the same lender and they will often do a desk top valuation for free rather than send a surveyor out to the property and charging you for it. It will most likely have a separate fixed penalty period of its own and run along side your current product. This is a feature of the product that will be advertised in the product guide. This feature may swing your decision regarding which product to choose because, some lenders / products will let you further advance as soon as a month after completion but you may pay handsomely for the privilege. The usual timescale is 3 to 6 months.

the mortgage works

Further Advance Application Form

(Release of equity from existing properties only. One application per account/property)

Decisions in principle are not available. All fully completed application forms to be submitted by post. Please telephone 08000 30 40 40 if you have any queries or would like to discuss a new application with an underwriter. Credit scoring techniques may be used in assessing the application.

Thank you for choosing The Mortgage Works

We aim to make the process of applying for a mortgage as simple as possible. To help, we have provided a handy checklist on the last page. Please complete the form in full and ensure that all the supporting documents are attached, otherwise delays may be experienced.

How to speed up your application:
- Please use **black ink** and **block capitals** throughout.
- Please ensure you answer all questions, if a question is not applicable write N/A.
- Ensure the Declaration in section 10 is signed by all applicants.
- If you wish to discuss any aspect of the application during processing please telephone on 08000 30 40 40 or email updates@themortgageworks.co.uk.
- Please send your completed form to: TMW New Business, The Mortgage Works, Portman House, Richmond Hill, Bournemouth BH2 6EP.

When we receive the application we will:
- Arrange for the valuation to be carried out.
- Take up any necessary references.
- Carry out a credit search and any other necessary checks.
- Return the originals of the supporting documentation to you as soon as possible.

Account number to be used for this further advance [ ]

Security address 11   STREET, HAZEL GROVE, Stockport
Postcode SK7

COMPLETION STATEMENT

Borrower: Mr
Customer Number: 320010-46444
Property Address: Stockport Road East, Bredbury, STOCKPORT, SK6

Completion Date: 12/06/2019

Advance Monies		£113495.00
Balance to be Deducted		£1015.00
Total Monies Received		£112480.00
Mortgage Redemption		
First Charge Together Commercial Finance Limited	£66110.50	
Total Amount to Repay Existing Charges	£66110.50	
Financial Advisors Fees		
Cheshire Mortgage Group	£0.00	
Balance of Mortgage Advance		£46369.50
Less Professional Fees		
	£0.00	
Other Fees		
Money Transfer Fees	£41.66	
VAT on Money Transfer Fees	£8.33	
EID Fee	£5.00	
VAT on EID Fee	£1.00	
Total Fees	£55.99	
Less Disbursements		
Total Disbursements	£0.00	
Balance of money due to you		£46313.51

CASE STUDY INTRODUCTION

The following case studies are based on my own previous projects. I have chosen them because they offer examples of a wide range of processes that were either purposefully planned or proved necessary later in the project. They all offer renovations, which are larger to some degree than others and they all involve finance. Where one property required the straightforward use of a BTL mortgage to initiate the purchase, another was facilitated by bridging finance. One property was flipped, where another had been renovated simply to rent out, probably with a remortgage involved and/or to release equity gained as a result of an increase in value, due to refurbishment.

There are examples involving valuers, structural engineers and building regulations. I have described my experiences of purchasing through an estate agency, joint agency and buying at auction. You will accompany me through projects that wouldn't raise an eyebrow and through other situations that would raise the hairs on the back of your neck. There are instances of projects using one catch all contractor and jobs where I have project managed several contractors.

Two of these case studies are cautionary tales and the other offers encouragement as to how simply the whole process can run. If I have missed any explicit details out of these anecdotes, it is because either I have covered them previously in the book or because they were not relevant to the story. The point of these case studies is to bring to life the information in the book, so you can imagine how the whole jigsaw fits together and visualise what it is like in the trenches at those times when you are greeted with adversity: but more importantly, it demonstrates how to overcome those various obstacles. Enjoy!

CASE STUDY 1

At this point in time, if I don't count an extremely slow renovation I completed whilst living in the property, I had finished three renovation projects. My first was a 3 bedroomed, 2 reception room, end terrace in the Tameside area of a Manchester. I had bought the house specifically to flip but things had not gone to plan. My first quote came from a company I remembered from my estate agent days and was £12,000 inc VAT just for the essential repairs, so I chanced my arm on another contractor that had popped into my memory. I knew he could do the whole job, which made sense, as I hadn't got a clue, apart from what I had gleaned from surveys and viewings 10 years previously. The property wasn't in the most saleable area and was situated over the side street from a conservative club. There was almost no back yard to speak of and the area was a far cry from Alderley Edge. After offering the property to market I received very little interest, so I decided to rent it out for 6 months and take stock from there; at least I'd be earning rental income. Before purchasing the property I had totally underestimated the costs of renovation (£16K) and given almost no thought to the fees involved (£10K). The contractor took twice as long as promised to finish the work and ultimately my profit would have been £5,000 if it had sold at the asking price; which clearly wasn't happening. Two tenants and 4 years later I sold the property and made £20,000 profit from an increase in market values locally, plus the rental income over the time. Oh and some very valuable lessons were learnt!

After this one came a small 2 bed terraced using the same contractor and it was done in 8 weeks and cost £10K plus fees. I'd bought it to rent out and have done so ever since. The next was a 3 bed semi in Stockport (Cheshire side) for my family and I to move into, which cost £17K. Again this was using the same contractor as before.

This contractor had been in the business for years and years . . . and years! He was also a qualified surveyor and what he didn't know about renovating property you could throw away in a sweet wrapper. When I came across the third property: a 2 bedroom, 2 reception room, very large end terrace property in Poynton, Cheshire. I called the director (Walter) and went through it with him. He said, "Chris you know what your doing now. Get the offer accepted and we'll go cost it up". So I did and we did. The first reception room was very small and had previously been a shop front. The second reception room was big and the kitchen was in 4 quarters: one was an empty brick room, the second was a tiny dilapidated kitchen of sorts, the third was empty and the fourth was a grotty downstairs W/C. This kitchen had been extended in the recent past and so had a lot of potential. At the top of the very steep stairs were two double bedrooms and a modest bathroom. The bathroom was at the end of a passage angled to avoid a chimney breast, which had been part of the original larger bedroom that you would have had to walk through to enter the bathroom originally. The main bedroom was large and had access to a fixed stairway leading to a boarded loft, featuring a Velux window facing out to the rear. There was a tiny space for off-road parking at the front and a side passage that was communally owned for access to the rest of the adjoining properties. Off this passage at the rear of the house was an overgrown, ample-sized garden.

Immediately turning to sold prices on Rightmove I found that only recently a 2 bed property on the same row had sold for £220K. I estimated the work costs and fees to be around £30K and thought that between my brother and I we could make £30K (assuming the market increased a little).

I chanced my arm with an offer of £165,000 and the vendors accepted. I thought this was a little quick and that raised alarm bells but this turned out to be due to a sale that had fallen through because of an adverse survey that had raised structural concerns. The sellers turned to their buildings insurance who investigated the claims and found that the signs of movement were historical. They had the crack monitored and secured the situation with straps and ties on the gable end (which was substantial in size). So these vendors were motivated and the work involved in restoring this property had been too much for the residentially motivated viewers who had viewed previously.

We got Walt in and were surprised to learn that it was going to take a little more investment than the original estimate of £15K to do the place up. It transpired that it was going to be a £25K job and with the fees being about £15K, this would leave us with about £7K each, if we got the full asking price. The job was starting to look a lot less appealing! I had wrongly assumed that the loft room was just in need of tarting up to create a legitimate third bedroom and would make us a pretty penny or two on top. However, Walt advised that the joists had to be replaced and this was a big job. Also, we needed to move the stairs so that it had separate access; On top of this building regs were required. I asked how much this would all cost and it came to an extra £20K (cheap for a loft conversion but not cheap compared to the original plan). So the entire cost would be £45K renovation and £15K in fees: in total £225K. However, for a 3 bedroomed property the agent estimated £250K-255K if finished to a high spec. Now we could be looking at our £30K profit again (optimistic as ever).

Now we needed to find our deposit as well as half the fees and the renovation money. This was a huge ask! Fortunately my brother had just sold a small business he was tired of running, so he stumped up half the money from that and I'd recently remortgaged a couple of renovations that I'd rented out, so also had residual cash in savings. The rest of the renovation fund was coming from my rental incomes and any other avenue I could find.

The mortgage product we were forced to take (because I had poor SA302s) and Jamie's weren't exactly effulgent, was a 5 year fixed fee with higher than normal interest rates (4.89%), as we could only afford to put down a deposit on an 80% LTV product. Half the reason the fees were so high was because we had to factor in a £7979.70 redemption penalty if we sold in the first year; the mortgage payments were £541.95 PCM.

FEES:

Survey £400

Purchasing solicitor £1000

Mortgage payments (6 months) £3250

Stamp duty (old rates) £1200

Fixed penalty £8000

Selling solicitor £900

Estate agent £2550

Total £17300

This just goes to show how I still hadn't got my figures down pat yet. I hadn't factored in a rental finders fee nor estimated the fees I'd planned for correctly. I was already more than £2K over budget and because I hadn't estimated the amount of work properly, my profits were not going to be fantastic after a shed load of work. The trouble was that we both felt pot committed and there were no other projects about, so we dived in head first.

THE RENOVATION

I was advised that planning wasn't necessary because we weren't putting in a window to the front of the loft conversion but we were required to seek building regs.

Plus a structural engineer needed to be consulted not only with regards to the loft but also the 2nd reception room that we were knocking through to create an open plan kitchen. In addition, we were going to create a utility room for a washing machine, dryer and fridge and then upscale the W/C and create a cloak room. We also needed to remove the giant shop window (with ivy growing on the inside) and replace it with a standard sized one. The chimney was twisted and so we elected to remove it and prop the inside breasts with lintels where necessary. Walt cleverly used the bricks from the chimney to fill in the gap where the shop window had been replaced with a smaller new one. The loft needed to have its joists removed and replaced with 7" load bearing joists, a second rear Velux window installed and the loft staircase had to be ripped out and replaced, partially into the space of the second bedroom. This second bedroom, although still just about a double, had to have its adjoining passage wall straightened out, which meant moving the bathroom door and removing the passage dwelling part of the chimney breast. This was all before the actual interior could be subjected to the usual renovation processes.

These processes included: re-plumbing, rewiring, plastering, new kitchen and bathroom etc etc. This was quite a job!

The works rolled on and as usual with Walt as with probably most builders, a week or two would sail by while his men were on other jobs or weather problems struck etc etc and it took twice as long as we'd originally envisaged. On top of this I was trying to liaise with Walt, the builders, the structural engineer and the building regs officer, I was losing all my enthusiasm and regretting the whole affair.

Side note: do not make your final payment to the builders until all the i's and t's are dotted and crossed as you will spend an unnecessary amount of time chasing them to get the last bits of paintwork sorted or a certificate that is still outstanding etc. In this case that time was 3 months!

The big day came minus some rogue dots and crosses and the house looked great. There was a building regs certificate we were waiting for; some damp patches due to painting while the plaster was still wet; some sealing to finish off and some of the joinery had moved away from the wall due to heat expansion; but it was good enough to sell.

Side note: it turned out that we also needed to get communicating smoke alarms on all three floors and fire doors for every exit leading from the loft conversion, to the front door. This had not been communicated to us by anyone and was a 'nice' little extra cost and waiting period we needed to endure before getting our regs.

The house was in a popular area of a popular district and ready to go to the first viewer. The agents came round and valued it at tops £275,000 and we were dancing around like highland flingers; so it went on the market for that.

Unfortunately, the house on the other end of the terrace came to market at the same time but on the upside ours was better and theirs had a funny lay out; guess who sold theirs first? It wasn't us! Apparently his larger dining room was more desirable. After this every viewer who came gave one excuse after the other for not offering: the stairs were too steep, the window in the kitchen hadn't got the optimum view for washing up at, the location wasn't ideal??? (they knew where it was when they booked the viewing) and the biggest negative was this small front room even though we had planned the living space to be the open plan 2nd reception room / kitchen. Time was getting away from us and we did what we should have done in the first place and got the place rented out; to our financial advisor of all people. Karen had been held up on a new build she was buying and liked the area; certainly more than her parents' house. She covered our mortgage and showed viewers around enthusiastically. When she finally left 6 months later we were forced to find more tenants and we just wanted to sell. The agents we were with didn't have a lettings service so we had to get another in to find us the tenant and they would only do this if we put the house for sale with them too. In the end we did a joint agency and we started to earn £150 each in rental income. Eventually we got an offer of £250K. We had reduced the price a couple of times to try and get that sale and this seemed fair now. We had actually had a similar offer right at the start of marketing but compared to our asking price it seemed cheeky; but not in hindsight! This offer was cash from a property they had sold and they were eager to move. But then it happened! They got a homebuyers report. I could see this going down the tube fast and it duly did. As soon as the surveyor had commented on 100 things be it favourable or not, the buyers were convinced it was falling down and no amount of reasoning would dissuade them from pulling out. Back to the drawing board. Eventually we found another buyer and agreed a sale at £250,000. They also got a homebuyers report and we were forced for no good reason to drop the price by £2000. They eventually completed so a 'swift' year and a half after we'd started the project we had eventually brought a conclusion to our project and left with a 'grand' profit of £12,000 each and a truck load of experience. OUCH!

ADDENDUM

Just before we found our eventual buyer I had chanced upon a house not far from my own that I really fancied buying to let out. It was a 2 bedroomed, 2 reception room terrace style semi detached on at £130K and a sale had just fallen through on it so she was keen to sell (in fact we knew each other). The house had originally been put on the market a year before, so was still on at last year's prices and the house next door had come on at £140K in a similar condition; £10K immediate equity. The trouble was that my money was tied up in the Poynton house. I had presumed Poynton would sell quickly and if not I could release some equity from it via a remortgage or further advance. Assuming that Jamie wouldn't mind, I embarked on the purchase of said house. Then the Poynton house didn't sell and I was starting to panic. I couldn't drum up any money from any other ventures so I went for the remortgage. My brother wasn't ecstatic about this as he was gaining nothing and not only that, it also meant that we would have to pay the giant fixed rate penalty, plus it meant that I was taking on another one, although this one wasn't too severe as I was only taking a 2 year fixed rate. After the surveyor had done his valuation on the Poynton house, I received the report - it was damning and the lender refused to even put a valuation on it. Structural defects, illegal loft conversion, possible progression of movement and a mention of a previous survey. Now the previous vendors to myself had had all the work sorted and there was found to be no structural problem; also how did he know the loft was illegal without an internal investigation, which would have proved otherwise? He also wasn't happy with the length of crack monitoring that the insurance company had done. I contacted the agent and asked why they had given private documents to the surveyor without my permission, but they denied it.

Suddenly, I realised what had happened. The buyers' surveyor had been doing a homebuyers report and I'd offered the buyers all the paperwork to prove all was well and above board, along with my other certificates and reports. They had handed them over to the homewrecker (I mean homebuyer surveyor) and as unbelievable bad luck would have it, he had run into my remortgage surveyor on the same day at the Poynton property. The homewrecker had unlawfully (in my opinion) imparted his 'knowledge' of all the things that had been wrong with the property when I bought it, without telling him that they had been rectified. My remortgage surveyor put this down in his report, without checking the veracity of the information and hence, the lenders refused to lend me any money. I was then forced to appeal this decision. The super annoying thing about the homebuyer report was that this surveyor was away with the fairies. He mentioned that he couldn't inspect the loft but stated that the joists were not standard for a conversion. He hadn't even looked at them: he'd just made it up! He also mentioned that there was no water source in the downstairs W/C and to prove this he had supplied a photo in his report which featured the water source I had had installed that he claimed wasn't there!!!

The remortgage surveyor then reappraised the case over about a month and concluded that he was happy with my appeal, except for the length of crack monitoring time done and said I must get a structural engineer to re measure and compare to the old results. They were favourable thank goodness and in the meantime a kind relative fronted me the money, so I was able to purchase the other house, do it up, gain equity, remortgage it and pay him back in a timely manner. Sometimes being a property developer is less than straight forward. You need to be creative, organised and damned dogged in your resolve; but it will pay off in the end.

Engineer's Report

Our Reference	**IFS-AGE-SUB-14-0051797**
Claim Reference	**HG14032970**
Prepared for	**Ageas Insurance Limited**

Claim Details:

Report Date	01 July 2014
Policyholder	**Exec of Groome**
Address	Road, Stockport, Cheshire, SK12

InFront-innovation is a trading name of InFront Solutions Ltd. Registered in England, no 03730163
Web Address: www.infront-innovation.com

ENGINEERS REPORT   Road, Stockport

REQUIREMENTS

In view that the damage to the property is considered to be as a result of an insured event, a valid claim arises under the terms of policy cover, subject to the applicable excess.

The cause of movement appears to be the result of water escaping into the ground from leaking drains (or from other sources) and site investigations will shortly be undertaken to test the drainage in the vicinity of the damage for leakage.

Defects found to the drainage system associated with the subsidence damage will require repair following which the property may need to monitored to confirm stability and a further claim update will be provided following the completion of site investigations. Should monitoring indicate that the movement is progressive, then further site investigations will be instructed.

Provided the property stabilises as expected, no foundation stabilisation works are considered necessary, with structural repairs of the superstructure being required only, together with internal redecoration of the damaged rooms.

Generally cracks 3mm wide or less will be filled. Where the cracks are wider than 3mm, but less than 5mm the underlying brickwork or blockwork will be exposed and prior to making good the plaster finishes the cracking will be covered with expanded metal lathe. Where cracks are 5mm across or wider, some form of bed joint reinforcement will be introduced.

Engineer
InFront Innovation Subsidence Management Services

MONITORING

CRACK MONITORING
for Subsidence Management Services

Road, , Stockport, Cheshire, SK12

Client:	Subsidence Management Services
Client Contact:	
Claim Number:	HG14032
Client Reference:	IFS-AGE-SUB-14-
Policy Holder:	Miss
Report Date:	19 February 2015
Our Ref:	M36

SubsNetuk

RICS Home Surveys...

RICS HomeBuyer Report...

Property address	Road Poynton Stockport Cheshire SK12
Client's name	Miss KM Mr JJ
Date of inspection	27th January 2017

Connells
SURVEY & VALUATION

RICS — the mark of property professionalism worldwide

F Inside the property

F7 Woodwork (for example, staircase and joinery)

Internal woodwork comprises of timber doors, stairs and skirting boards.

The skirting boards in contact with the areas of dampness described in section E4 will require treatment/ replacement in conjunction with those works and condition rating.

Internal woodwork is generally in satisfactory condition with no serious disrepair evident. Some localised repairs may well be needed when the present owner removes furniture and fittings.

The main staircase is a straight flight which is traditional for the age of the home. The retention of handrails for safety is advised. The staircase has no excessive movement to the treads or risers although maintenance to glue and screw the timbers with removal of the floor covering is advised.

Internal Decorations

The internal decorations are generally satisfactory, although you should allow for some marking to be revealed when the present owners remove their fixtures and fittings, and that some localised redecoration will be required. We expect that you have assessed the adequacy of decorations for your own purposes.

Condition Rating 1.

F8 Bathroom fittings

The ground floor Toilet does not have ventilation. There is also some distance to a wash hand basin. Although there is an exemption from a wash hand basin when close to the kitchen or other fitting in this case a suitable wash hand basin would be prudent.

The bathroom comprises a white suite with a bath with shower over off the central heating system, wash hand basin and toilet.

The fittings are in functional visual condition but are not tested in accordance with the Description of Service requirements.

Condition Rating 3.

Seals surrounding the sanitary fittings are a source of water penetration. These should be checked regularly and renewed as necessary.

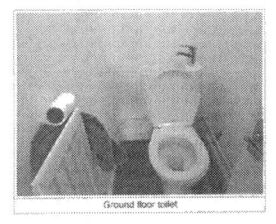

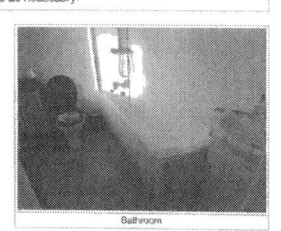

[Handwritten note: There is one on the toilet]

Ground floor toilet | Bathroom

Property address: Road, Poynton, Stockport, Cheshire, SK12

RICS HomeBuyer Report

F Inside the property

Limitations to inspection

Fitted floor coverings, items of furniture and storage restricted the inspection of the main areas.

We were unable to see the underside of the staircase.

The original roof void has been converted to provide additional accommodation and all of the roof construction is now concealed.

The use of plasterboard linings on walls prevents inspection of the masonry behind

F1 Roof structure

A staircase has been provided to the roof void. The roof void is now fully lined to the floor, ceiling and walls. There is plaster encasement of roof supports and these cannot be inspected

There is no access to the lower roof eaves. Suitable access hatches would be prudent to allow for maintenance access and also assessment of structural condition. The provision of thermal insulation in the roof void and ceiling is not known. The presence of 'pattern staining' on the ceiling contours suggests the roof was not thermally insulated as part of the conversion works.

The original roof void has been converted to provide additional accommodation. This conversion is not to habitable room standards. The floor has not been strengthened to current structural design requirements for stability. The floor is a 'platform' style of construction with timbers laid over the original ceiling joists. The roof void is not suitable for use as a bedroom or for permanent habitable purposes

Not inspected.

F2 Ceilings

Ceilings are a mix of lath and plaster and plasterboard

Unevenness and cracking was noted in some areas but this is not unusual for a property of this type and age. Repair works will be required when redecorating.

Condition Rating 2.

F3 Walls and partitions

Internal walls and partitions are a mixture of solid and lightweight construction. These are partly dry-lined internally

The property appears to be affected by serious structural movement evidenced by cracking to the rear two storey extension junction. This needs further investigation from a Structural Engineer to establish the cause. You should request advice on the remedial repairs needed and the cost.

A potentially load-bearing wall has been removed between the former rear living room and the alterations to the present kitchen. The loads from above should have been provided with some form of support, although this is now concealed within the fabric of the building and we are unable to confirm either its adequacy or existence. Whilst we saw no signs of distress during the inspection, your legal adviser should contact the local authority Building Control Department to confirm that the works were undertaken with their knowledge and consent. See Section 11.

There is a plaster crack in the rear wall of the front living room, which will require suitable filling.

Property address: Road, Poynton, Stockport, Cheshire, SK12

RICS HomeBuyer Report

LENDER'S COPY

KentReliance

Report and valuation

| Applicants | Mr C | | Application no | 0 |
| Property Address | Road Poynton Stockport Cheshire SK12 | | | |

Did the property appear to be tenanted at the time of inspection? Yes ☐ No [X]

1 Description of Property

House [X]　Bungalow ☐　Purpose built flat ☐　Converted flat ☐　Other ☐ Details
Detached ☐　Semi detached ☐　End terrace [X]　Mid terrace ☐　Other ☐ Details

If Flat
Floor(s) on which located ☐　No. of floors in block ☐　No. of units in block ☐　Lift provided Yes ☐ No ☐
Above commercial premises　Yes ☐　No ☐　If Yes, please give details in General Remarks
Was the property built for the public sector, e.g. local authority, military, police? Yes ☐ No [X] If Yes, please give details in General Remarks

Part Commercial:
Is the residential use greater than 40%　Yes ☐　No [X]
What percentage of the floor area could be classified as the living accommodation? 100 %
Year property built 1910

2 Properties less than 10 years old / New build properties

Is the property under 10 years old? Yes ☐ No [X]
If Yes, please detail what warranty cover is in place:
NHBC ☐　Checkmate ☐　Premier Guarantee ☐　Building Life Plan ☐　LABC ☐
Is this a New Build property? Yes ☐ No ☐
If Yes, have you seen the CML Disclosure of Incentives form Yes ☐ No ☐ If Yes, date of form
Please give details of builder's name, state of construction and whether a re-inspection is necessary in General Remarks

3 Accommodation

No of Floors	Living Room(s)	Bedroom(s)	Kitchen(s)	Bathroom(s)	Separate WC's	Cellar(s)	Other rooms	Garage(s)	Garage Space	Out-buildings	Garden
3	1	2	1	1	1	0	2	0	1	0	1

If other rooms, give details: Utility room, loft room / attic (not habitable space).

Services

No tests were carried out of the services which are connected to the property
Does the property have: Mains gas [X]　Mains electricity [X]　Mains water [X]
Central heating: Full [X]　Part ☐　None ☐
Type of central heating: Gas [X]　Electric ☐　Solid fuel ☐　Other ☐
Drainage: Mains [X]　Septic tank ☐　Cess pool ☐

5 Construction

Is the property of traditional construction? Yes [X] No ☐
Main walls: Majority solid brick, part cavity brick (circa 255-275mm).
Main roof: Majority pitched slates, part flat felt/asphalt.
Garage: N/A no garage.
Outbuildings: N/A - no outbuildings.

6 Tenure

Freehold [X]　Leasehold ☐
If Leasehold: Unexpired term ___ years
Ground rent £ ___ p.a.　Service charge £ ___ p.a.

Page 1 of 4

LENDER'S COPY

7 Roads

Adopted [X]   Private [ ]

If Private:
Made up [ ]   Partially made [ ]   Unmade [ ]

8 Condition of property

Is the property affected by subsidence, settlement, heave or landslip?	Yes [X]	No [ ]
Is the property built on a steeply sloping site?	Yes [ ]	No [X]
Is there any evidence of subsidence, settlement, heave or landslip in the immediate vicinity?	Yes [ ]	No [X]
Are there any trees in influencing distance of the property?	Yes [ ]	No [X]

If Yes, please provide details in Sections 9 or 10 as appropriate

9 Essential repairs

(Please list and indicate whether an undertaking is considered sufficient or whether a retention is recommended)

No matters to raise.

Is a retention recommended   Yes [ ]   No [X]
If Yes, amount of retention   £

10 Specialist Reports

Are any Specialist Reports required?   Yes [ ]   No [X]

If Yes, please tick as appropriate
Damp and Timber [ ]   Electrical [ ]   Drains [ ]   Roof [ ]   Structural Engineers [ ]
Mining [ ]   Arboricultural [ ]   Other [ ]   Detail

11 General remarks

(If new property state Builder's name, stage of construction and whether reinspection is necessary)

The property has been declined as unsuitable for mortgage purposes as it does not satisfy the Lender's 'core requirements' in terms of confirmed structural stability, future insurability (i.e. illegal loft conversion and possible progressive movement) and marketability as a result. The structural engineer's previous recommendations contained within his report (09/06/2014) to investigate possibly progressive foundation movement and therefore a possible requirement for underpinning plus a recommendation for the installation of replacement wall ties and works to the presently illegal/non-compliant loft conversion works have not been confirmed / documented having been completed to satisfactory standard and a certificate of structural

12 Suitability of property for letting purposes

Is this a Buy to Let application?   Yes [X]   No [ ]

If No, proceed to Section 13

(i) Is the property subject to an existing tenancy?   Yes [ ]   No [X]
If Yes, provide details in Additional Comments section

(ii) Is the property of a type which there is a steady demand for letting purposes?   Yes [X]   No [ ]
If No, provide details in Additional Comments section

(iii) Is the property situated in an area where there is a steady demand for letting purposes?   Yes [X]   No [ ]
If No, provide details in Additional Comments section

Additional Comments

Whilst the property is a type (i.e. terrace house) which readily lets locally, the possibly progressive structural movement and non-compliant alterations render the property as unsuitable for mortgage and hence letting purposes.

LENDER'S COPY

Rental Valuation

Assuming a 6 month Assured Shorthold Tenancy what is the property's realistic rental value per calender month?

Furnished £850 Unfurnished £850

13 Valuation

Is the property being purchased on a Shared Ownership basis? Yes ☐ No [X]

If Yes, % share _____ Please note that the Present Condition valuation figure should be for the whole property.

Present condition	£250,000
Essential repairs/construction completed	£
Gross external floor area	117 sq metres
Valuation for buildings insurance	£170,000

14 Recommendation

Is the property recommended as a suitable security for mortgage purpose? Yes [X] No ☐

If No, please give details in General Remarks

Valuer's declaration

I certify that I have personally inspected the property described in this report. I also confirm that I have no financial or other interests in the property and that the report has been prepared in accordance with Kent Reliance Banking Services Valuation Guidance Notes and the provisions of the RICS Valuation Standards.

By signing this report, I confirm that I hold a current registration under the RICS Registration Scheme.

Signed	530303 = 9623
Valuer's name and qualifications	FRICS ☐ MRICS [X] AssocRICS ☐
RICS Membership No.	0095439
Name and address of firm	Connells Survey & Valuation Ltd Macclesfield Office, c/o VMC, Cumbria House, 16-20 Hockliffe Street Leighton Buzzard LU7 1GN
Telephone number	01525 218637
Fax number	01525 218632
Email	CSBcc@connells.co.uk
Date of inspection	24/08/2016
Date of report	24/08/2016

Please provide photographs of front elevation, rear elevation, street scene, bathroom and kitchen.

Important notes for applicants

This is a copy of the mortgage valuation report, which has been prepared for OneSavings Bank plc ('us/we'). The sole purpose of the report is to enable us to assess the suitability of the proposed security and to decide on the amounts (if any) that can be advanced on mortgage.

Kent Reliance Banking Services have not instructed the Valuer to carry out a detailed inspection and the report is not a condition structural survey, nor is it a Homebuyers report, both of which would require a more detailed inspection.

This valuation has been undertaken in accordance with the RICS specification for residential mortgage valuation. It is quite possible that there are defects in the property which were not evident during the course of the limited inspection, or which the valuer has not disclosed, as they are not considered to materially affect the property's value.

You should not therefore, assume that if no defects are mentioned, the property is free from defect, nor should you assume the defects referred to (if any) are the only defects present in the property.

If you are proposing to purchase the property and you wish to be satisfied as to the condition of it, you must have a surveyors detailed inspection and report of your own before deciding to enter into a contract.

* See Continuation Page *

LENDER'S COPY

Kent**Reliance**

Report and valuation
Continuation Page

Applicants	Mr C	Application no	0
Property Address	Road, Poynton Stockport Cheshire SK12		

11. General remarks (continued)
adequacy/stability subsequently issued by the appropriately qualified professional person.

Whilst documentation was seen confirming that crack monitoring had been undertaken and a Certificate of Structural Adequacy issued (20/08/15) by the Subsidence Management Services Department of the applicant's insurers, this is considered inadequate in the circumstances. No confirmation of the issuer's professional qualifications is documented and given that other works were also identified as required (as above) during the original inspection by the appropriately qualified structural engineer in order to confirm structural stability and in order to rectify previous illegal / non-compliant alterations.

Consequently, we are unable to provide valuation or rental advice within our report.

...e property is located in an established residential area within reasonable access of amenities.

Work has been carried out involving the construction of extensions to the rear, the removal/alteration of a number of internal walls and the conversion of a former loft to residential use (currently non-compliant) which may require building Regulation approval or a Compliance Certificate from a Registered Installer. Legal Advisers should confirm that all necessary Notices have been served and Regulations complied with.

Any applicants are strongly advised to obtain their own more detailed reports in order to become fully conversant with the various repairs/improvements currently outstanding which are now required.

Flat roof coverings (i.e. to rear extensions have a limited life - circa 30% total plan area) and on-going repair and periodic replacement must be anticipated. It should be appreciated that felt covered flat roofs have limited life expectancy requiring regular maintenance, repair and renewal. Experience has shown that leaks can manifest themselves unpredictably.

Tests on the condition and safety of service installations (including the central heating system) prior to contract would be prudent.

PLEASE NOTE: The Valuer's address shown in this report is an Administration Centre only. The Valuer is locally based.

* End of Report *

Northern Structural Services
Civil & Structural Engineers

1 Prestbury Road
Macclesfield
SK10 1AU
Tel: 01625 425243
Fax: 01625 429714
Website: www.northernstructuralservices.co.uk

Your ref: Our ref: C11   //TMB/SB

Hazel Grove
Stockport
SK7

26th September 2016

Dear Mr

C11 — Clumber Road, Poynton

Following your recent instructions we visited the above property on 19th September 2016 to carry out a structural inspection and our comments are given below.

For the purpose of this report, all directions referred to are as when viewed from the front of the property. This survey is for your exclusive use and your professional advisers to whom liability in respect of the contents of this work would be limited. The report is based upon a visual inspection of the super structure as it stands, no openings have been formed in the super structure, nor have we checked for dampness.

The property was a left hand, end terrace domestic dwelling.

EXTERNAL

Front Elevation

This elevation was facing brick, which was stretcher bonded indicating cavity construction. Across this elevation is a canopy to the front door and the ground floor window. The roof was pitched. To the left side the coursing slopes down to the left. There were stone lintels over the first floor window. There has been some re-pointing above the flashing detail to the canopy.

There is an old stepped crack running up to the left from the top right corner of the canopy to the right side of the first floor window. The lower brickwork appears to be relatively new.

Reg Office: 1 Prestbury Road, Macclesfield, Cheshire SK10 1AU. Reg No 3597053 V A T No 286 0337 51
"Northern Structural Services" is the trading name of Northern Structural Services Limited

...ility & Toilet Room

There was a step down into this area. The floor was 'on solid' construction and slopes down towards the rear. There was cracking to the coving detail running around the left and rear edges of the ceiling.

First Floor

Front Bedroom

The floor was covered with carpet, which we were not able to lift, so we could not determine the direction of the floor joists. The floor was reasonably level. There was a chimney breast to the left side. There was a very fine crack to the left side of the rear wall near the light switch.

Rear Bedroom

The floor was covered with chipboard so we were not able to determine the direction of the floor joists. The floor was reasonably level. The left wall was studwork as was the front wall. There was a very fine vertical crack to the left wall above the top rear corner of the door.

Bathroom

This was to the rear left in the 2 storey extension. The floor was covered with lino so were not able to determine the direction of the floor joists. The floor was reasonably level.

Second Floor

A room has been created within the centre of the roof space. To the front and rear appear to be the outlines of the roof purlins encased in plasterboard. The front and rear walls are studwork and the ceiling reflects the roof slope.

CONCLUSIONS AND RECOMMENDATIONS

From the above, we would comment that there were signs of structural movement to the property. This is to be expected in a property of this type and age and was generally misalignment of wall and floor lines.

We would comment that we have previously visited this property in 2014 and since that time and some alterations have been undertaken. The front elevation has had brickwork added in place of the former shop front and some of the rear room areas beyond the kitchen have been opened up to create a more open plan feel to this property.

We have noted in our most recent observations that there are a number of cracks to the front elevation, side elevation and within the property and these have also been observed in 2014. We are also aware that following our initial report in 2014 insurance monitoring has been carried out to the property which concluded that any movement had ceased.

LENDER'S COPY

KentReliance

Report and valuation

Applicants	Mr C		Application no	0

Property Address	Road Poynton Stockport Cheshire SK12

Did the property appear to be tenanted at the time of inspection? Yes ☐ No ☒

1 Description of Property

House ☒ Bungalow ☐ Purpose built flat ☐ Converted flat ☐ Other ☐ Details ____
Detached ☐ Semi detached ☐ End terrace ☒ Mid terrace ☐ Other ☐ Details ____

If Flat

Floor(s) on which located ____ No. of floors in block ____ No. of units in block ____ Lift provided Yes ☐ No ☐

Above commercial premises Yes ☐ No ☐ If Yes, please give details in General Remarks

Was the property built for the public sector, e.g. local authority, military, police? Yes ☐ No ☒ If Yes, please give details in General Remarks

Part Commercial:

Is the residential use greater than 40%? Yes ☐ No ☒

What percentage of the floor area could be classified as the living accommodation? 100 %

Year property built 1910

2 Properties less than 10 years old / New build properties

Is the property under 10 years old? Yes ☐ No ☒

If Yes, please detail what warranty cover is in place:

NHBC ☐ Checkmate ☐ Premier Guarantee ☐ Building Life Plan ☐ LABC ☐

Is this a New Build property? Yes ☐ No ☐

If Yes, have you seen the CML Disclosure of Incentives form Yes ☐ No ☐ If Yes, date of form ____

Please give details of builder's name, state of construction and whether a re-inspection is necessary in General Remarks

3 Accommodation

No of Floors	Living Room(s)	Bedroom(s)	Kitchen(s)	Bathroom(s)	Separate WC's	Cellar(s)	Other rooms	Garage(s)	Garage Space	Out-buildings	Garden
3	1	2	1	1	1	0	2	0	1	0	1

If other rooms, give details: Utility room, attic room / occasional bedroom 3.

Services

No tests were carried out of the services which are connected to the property

Does the property have: Mains gas ☒ Mains electricity ☒ Mains water ☒
Central heating: Full ☒ Part ☐ None ☐
Type of central heating: Gas ☒ Electric ☐ Solid fuel ☐ Other ☐
Drainage: Mains ☒ Septic tank ☐ Cess pool ☐

5 Construction

Is the property of traditional construction? Yes ☒ No ☐

Main walls: Majority solid brick, part cavity brick (circa 255-275mm).
Main roof: Majority pitched slates, part flat felt/asphalt.
Garage: N/A no garage.
Outbuildings: N/A - no outbuildings.

6 Tenure

Freehold ☒ Leasehold ☐

If Leasehold: Unexpired term ____ years
Ground rent £ ____ p.a. Service charge £ ____ p.a.

Page 1 of 4

LENDER'S COPY

7 Roads

Adopted [X] Private [ ]

If Private:
Made up [ ] Partially made [ ] Unmade [ ]

8 Condition of property

Is the property affected by subsidence, settlement, heave or landslip?	Yes [X]	No [ ]
Is the property built on a steeply sloping site?	Yes [ ]	No [X]
Is there any evidence of subsidence, settlement, heave or landslip in the immediate vicinity?	Yes [ ]	No [X]
Are there any trees in influencing distance of the property?	Yes [ ]	No [X]

If Yes, please provide details in Sections 9 or 10 as appropriate

9 Essential repairs

(Please list and indicate whether an undertaking is considered sufficient or whether a retention is recommended)

No matters to raise.

Is a retention recommended   Yes [ ]   No [X]

If Yes, amount of retention   £

10 Specialist Reports

Are any Specialist Reports required?   Yes [ ]   No [X]

If Yes, please tick as appropriate

Damp and Timber [ ]   Electrical [ ]   Drains [ ]   Roof [ ]   Structural Engineers [ ]
Mining [ ]   Arboricultural [ ]   Other [ ]   Detail

11 General remarks

(If new property state Builder's name, stage of construction and whether reinspection is necessary)

For the accommodation, location and condition and given the recently completed comparable sales evidence in our possession, we are unable to justify a figure in excess of our valuation.

Our valuation reflects the general condition of the property in its present state, although certain repairs and/or improvements, which do not directly affect mortgageability, are required. Our valuation figure assumes vacant possession on completion.

The property is located in an established residential area within reasonable access of

12 Suitability of property for letting purposes

Is this a Buy to Let application?   Yes [X]   No [ ]

If No, proceed to Section 19

(i) Is the property subject to an existing tenancy?   Yes [ ]   No [X]
If Yes, provide details in Additional Comments section

(ii) Is the property of a type which there is a steady demand for letting purposes?   Yes [X]   No [ ]
If No, provide details in Additional Comments section

(iii) Is the property situated in an area where there is a steady demand for letting purposes?   Yes [X]   No [ ]
If No, provide details in Additional Comments section

Additional Comments

The property is of a type (i.e. terrace house) and in a location, within which properties currently let readily.

LENDER'S COPY

Rental Valuation

Assuming a 6 month Assured Shorthold Tenancy what is the property's realistic rental value per calender month?

Furnished £ 0   Unfurnished £ 0

13 Valuation

Is the property being purchased on a Shared Ownership basis?   Yes ☐   No ☒

If Yes, % share _____   Please note that the Present Condition valuation figure should be for the whole property.

Present condition	£ 0
Essential repairs/construction completed	£
Gross external floor area	117 sq metres
Valuation for buildings insurance	£ 0

14 Recommendation

Is the property recommended as a suitable security for mortgage purpose?   Yes ☐   No ☒

If No, please give details in General Remarks

Valuer's declaration

I certify that I have personally inspected the property described in this report. I also confirm that I have no financial or other interests in the property and that the report has been prepared in accordance with Kent Reliance Banking Services Valuation Guidance Notes and the provisions of the RICS Valuation Standards.

By signing this report, I confirm that I hold a current registration under the RICS Registration Scheme.

Signed	605012 - 9925
Valuer's name	
and qualifications	FRICS ☐ MRICS ☒ AssocRICS ☐
RICS Membership No.	8095
Name and address of firm	Connells Survey & Valuation Ltd Macclesfield Office, c/o VMS, Cumbria House, 16-20 Hockliffe Street Leighton Buzzard LU7 1GN
Telephone number	01525 218647
Fax number	01525 213632
Email	CSRco@connells.co.uk
Date of inspection	24/03/2016
Date of report	24/03/2016

Please provide photographs of front elevation, rear elevation, street scene, bathroom and kitchen.

Important notes for applicants

This is a copy of the mortgage valuation report, which has been prepared for OneSavings Bank plc ('us/we'). The sole purpose of the report is to enable us to assess the suitability of the proposed security and to decide on the amounts (if any) that can be advanced on mortgage.

Kent Reliance Banking Services have not instructed the Valuer to carry out a detailed inspection and the report is not a condition structural survey, nor is it a Homebuyers report, both of which would require a more detailed inspection.

This valuation has been undertaken in accordance with the RICS specification for residential mortgage valuation. It is quite possible that there are defects in the property which were not evident during the course of the limited inspection, or which the valuer has not disclosed, as they are not considered to materially affect the property's value.

You should not therefore, assume that if no defects are mentioned, the property is free from defect, nor should you assume the defects referred to (if any) are the only defects present in the property.

If you are proposing to purchase the property and you wish to be satisfied as to the condition of it, you must have a surveyors detailed inspection and report of your own before deciding to enter into a contract.

* See Continuation Page *

LENDER'S COPY

Kent**Reliance**

Report and valuation
Continuation Page

Applicants	Mr D	Application no	0
Property Address	Poynton Stockport Cheshire SK**		

11. General remarks (continued)
amenities.

The property shows signs of longstanding movement. Within the confines of our inspection, this does not appear to be progressive and saleability should not be adversely affected. No specialist report is required in this instance.

Work has been carried out involving the construction of extensions to the rear, the removal/alteration of a number of internal walls and the conversion of a former loft to residential use (loft room / occasional bedroom) which may require Building Regulation approval or a Compliance Certificate from a Registered Installer. Legal Advisers should confirm that all necessary Notices have been served and Regulations complied with.

For the purposes of our valuation, it is assumed that the property will comply with all relevant Health and Safety Regulations prior to letting.

Any applicants are strongly advised to obtain their own more detailed reports in order to become fully conversant with the various repairs/improvements currently outstanding which are now required.

Flat roof coverings (i.e. to rear extensions) have a limited life - circa 30% total plan area) and on-going repair and periodic replacement must be anticipated. It should be appreciated that felt covered flat roofs have limited life expectancy requiring regular maintenance, repair and renewal. Experience has shown that leaks can manifest themselves unpredictably.

Tests on the condition and safety of service installations (including the central heating system) prior to contract would be prudent.

This amended report has been prepared as documentation has subsequently been received confirming structural stability at the property including confirmation that both lender and underwriter are satisfied that alterations undertaken (including loft conversion) have been completed to their satisfaction.

PLEASE NOTE: The Valuer's address shown in this report is an Administration Centre only. The Valuer is locally based.

* End of Report *

subsidence
management

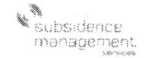

CERTIFICATE OF STRUCTURAL ADEQUACY

Name of Client:
Address of Property: Road, Stockport, Cheshire, SK12
Terms of appointment: We were appointed to proactively project manage this claim within the terms of your Building Insurance Policy

Our Reference: IFS-AGE-SUB-14-0051797   Insurer Claim Reference: HG14032970

1. **Brief description of damage to the property.**
   Damage was noted to the Living Room, Dining Room, Under Stairs Cupboard, Kitchen, Stairway, Landing, Front Bedroom, Main 1st Floor Landing and Front Elevation.

2. **Cause of damage to the property.**
   This is to certify that, as required by our terms of appointment, we have appraised the property as regards to the above damage, which in our professional opinion has been caused by subsidence as a result of consolidation of the ground below the foundations of the property.

3. **Property Stabilisation Measures.**
   Crack monitoring was undertaken which confirmed that the property was sufficiently stable to allow repairs to commence.

4. **Superstructure Repairs/Redecoration.**
   Repair work has been undertaken to the property. The work consisted generally of superstructure crack repairs and redecorations. The work was completed by The Forshaw Group and completed in August 2015

This certificate is for the sole benefit of the above named client and may not be relied on by any other person whatsoever. Transfer of the benefit of this certificate to any party other than the client to whom it is addressed will only be permitted with the written permission of Subsidence Management Services. Before agreeing to any transfer of benefit Subsidence Management Services may require to re-inspect the property, for which a fee may be charged.

Signed: Date: 16th November 2015

Print Name   Position: Senior Technical Claims Partner

For and on behalf of Innovation Property (UK) Limited

Address: Yarmouth House, 1300 Parkway, Solent Business Park, Whiteley, Hampshire, PO15 7AE

This certificate is a considered professional opinion and is not a warranty or guarantee as regards the works undertaken, and no liability shall attach to us except to the extent that we have failed to exercise reasonable skill, care and diligence in the provision of our services under our Terms of Appointment. This certificate is not a certificate of design of construction as defined in The Building Act 1984 and The Building (Approved Inspectors etc.) Regulations.

We have only examined and addressed the problems with the building relating to this particular episode of subsidence. We have not extended our inspection to other parts of the structure and therefore cannot comment on their adequacy or otherwise.

meridian consult

Tel. 01785 859200
Fax 01785 859210
Email: @meridianconsult.co.uk
Web: www.meridianconsult.co.uk

Hazel Grove
Stockport
Cheshire
Sk7

Address: **Meridian Consult Ltd**
Unit 4 Sugnall Business Centre
Sugnall
Eccleshall
Staffordshire
ST21 6NF

Date 18th October 2016

Your ref:
Our ref:

Dear Sir,

Re Loft alterations and internal alterations at   Road Poynton

I can confirm the works covered by the initial notice were as follows:-

1. The replacement of the existing loft floor with a new structural floor comprising of 175 x 75 timbers graded timbers spanning on to bolted bearers to gable and party walls and the provision of rafter triangulation ties. At the same time the existing stair position was moved from the front bedroom and repositioned off the landing area and a new stair was provided. Due to change in configuration new studs were erected to form improved access and the stair opening was newly trimmed out as part of the new floor construction.

2. The thermal upgrading works of the loft area room as the existing linings were removed as part of the upgrade works.

3. Structural openings were created on the ground floor between the back mid room and rear room, which involved the provision of new structural steel beams to a structural engineers design. A new foundation was formed to the steel bearing pier adjacent to the party wall.

4. An additional opening was created to the first floor adjacent to the existing bathroom area. For which a substantial steel beam was provided over.

5. A number of doors were replaced with fire doors to improve the existing 3 storey means of escape situation.

6. The gathered chimney stack was removed within the loft area and as this was removed full height out of the roof no additional support was required.

Registered in Cardiff No. 4670165
Registered Office: Unit 4 Sugnall Business Centre, Eccleshall, Staffordshire ST21 6NF

meridian consult

7. Four inspections were made during the course of the works to inspect the structural alterations and loft floor replacement.

8. A final certificate was issued on 5th September 2016 – which is the Approved Inspector's equivalence to a Local Authority Completion Certificate. Approved Inspectors are persons authorised under the Building Act 1984 to carry out building control work in England and Wales. Some question has been made as to the wording in respect to the following statement ' This certificate is evidence (but not conclusive evidence) that the requirements specified in it have been complied with'. This is a standard wording on all final certificates and is also included on Local Authority Completion Certificates.

   Limited numbers are inspections are made on a project and the role of a Building Control Surveyor is not to act as a Clerk of Works or Quality Inspectorate, so not every element of a project is inspected and there is a reliance on the contractor to carry out works in accordance with relevant standards and this wording reflects this fact.

There were a number of other property upgrades and renovation works carried out to the property not covered by the notice.

I hope this clarifies the situation

Yours faithfully

Building Control Surveyor
Mobile - 07793

Registered in Cardiff No: 4670165
Registered Office: Unit 4 Sugnall Business Centre, Eccleshall, Staffordshire. ST21 6NF

CASE STUDY 2

When my partner and I first met we each had a home of our own. Time passed and we decided to try living together. Juliette moved in with me and after the test of whether I was a hideous beast or not had been completed, she decided to move in with me permanently anyway.

Her house was in above average condition at the time and she found a local girl with two children (who had just split from her partner) to move in. Supported largely by her ex-partner, they stayed in situ for the following 7 years. She then decided to try and make a go of the relationship again but in Australia and off they went.

We knew that the house was going to need work as not only had she worn everything down with family life, on top of that the décor was now well out of date. It had become apparent that her house was now a refurb job! We initially thought of renovating the house and selling it, using the proceeds to buy two properties. She had always overpaid on her repayment mortgage and so the equity had built up. Then it dawned on me that there was no point in getting two houses when we could rent this one out newly renovated and buy one other.

She only owed about £65K; done up it was worth between £125K and £135K. In its current condition it was worth £100K-£110K but spending what I assessed to be £10K-£15K worth of work, with negligible fees, she stood to profit around£20K. The house was double glazed and central heated, the boiler had been replaced a year ago and so this was a comparatively easy renovation:

Rip out the stuff you don't want
Little bit of re wiring and down lights installed
Dot 'n' dab and re-skim
Put in a new kitchen and bathroom (bought on interest free, buy now pay in 12 months credit at B&Q) with some nice extras
Paint
New flooring

The actual cost came to £13K and took a couple of months as our builder ex neighbour and friend, Ciaran, was doing it alongside other jobs. We got a plasterer off mybuilder.com who was fast, cheap and the quality was excellent! As you will see in the next case study, portals can't always be trusted! And Ciaran (the builder) got his mate in to do the electrics.

The agent that came to view said it was worth £135K tops and the rental valuation was £650 tops only because the finish was so nice. She rented the house out next day to the first viewer for the top rent valuation.

Then it was time for the remortgage. The valuer had been instructed and I insisted on meeting him at the property myself and for good reason. When a lender says that they are instructing a local surveyor, local can mean from 20 miles away. I'm sure they inspect a lot of properties and have been around the area before but the nuances in valuation from one end of a street to another can prove challenging for a local estate agency let alone some dude who lives 20 miles away.

Side note: about 5 years ago I was remortgaging two houses that were 6 doors away from each other. The first house had been lovingly renovated and benefited from 2 bedrooms and 2 reception rooms with a kitchen built into a small extension. It had a double and a single bedroom and a fantastic 4 piece bathroom (a stand out feature in a small 2 bedder). The second property had almost the same foot print but without the kitchen extension leaving just one reception room; essentially I had done a basic refurb for rental purposes. I met the surveyor at the second, less high spec property and the tenant met the other surveyor at the higher end spec property. By rights the nicer, larger property should have been valued higher but it was valued £5000 less. Different surveyors have different opinions and to be fair, don't always get it right. Being on site and talking the situation through with the surveyor, who had travelled 18 miles to value it, ensured that he came to the correct decision. I'm not saying I swayed the man unduly but both clearly needed a little added information and had one surveyor seen both of them, there would have been consistency at least.

In this instance, the surveyor turned out to actually live locally. He walked around and completed his usual investigations and I made polite conversation. I mentioned I had just had two estate agents around to value the property (which I had) and the surveyor's curiosity proved too much for him. He asked what they had said and I was completely honest. Valuation for sale £135K and a rental valuation of £650 PCM. When I enquired he advised me that he wasn't at liberty to disclose his findings, but he was a nice man and said he thought that the valuation figure seemed reasonable but the rent maybe a little high. When the report came back in he had valued up to £135K and valued the rent down to £625, which was his opinion and in most cases would have been right, but we got the £650 rental because the property was done really nicely.

With the £135K valuation and the rental calculation fitting the lenders criterion, they lent Juliette 75% LTV. £135K X 75% = £101,250. This money was used to pay back her existing mortgage and left her with £20,000 change after taking into account the renovation costs.

This is an example of everything going right with a BTL / renovation project with a remortgage tacked on for good measure. If the last case study put you right off property then this one should pull you right back in.

CASE STUDY 3

Jamie and I had spotted a house not far from some other rentals I own and it was featured in Edward Mellor's auction catalogue. The property to my recollection was a basic 2 bed terrace needing updating throughout and was at the Hyde end of Dukinfield with a guide price of £32,000. Now I knew this house was going to garner a lot of interest at such an enticing price but at auction you never know which house will gain the most attention. I ascertained that it was probably worth £90K tops when done so if it sold in the £60,000s it was a good buy. Not necessarily to flip but to do up, rent out and remortgage would have been just peachy. There was also some allotment land in the the middle of a housing estate, not too far away from us, on at a guide of £5000 that was certainly worth a punt. The access was probably not wide enough for a new multiple house building project but maybe a passable one for one house on a fantastic plot. I also fancied starting a storage unit business and at £5K why not have a pop?

Jamie took our sister to the auction and he registered at the administration desk. I followed them half an hour later and said hello to an old colleague who was in charge of their auction department. I met up with the the others and had a scan through the auction pack to see if there was anything glaringly bad about the two lots. They seemed fine and so we went in and endured the slow burning start to the auction. Jamie and Christina got bored and so they left me to hold the fort and almost immediately after their departure the auction sped up nicely. I was just happy to be sat down away from responsibility for an afternoon. The 2 bed house went for £75K in the end so was of no interest at that point. The land went for a staggering £35K to some friends of a friend. It turned out they needed car parking space for a local business; but the high price they paid demonstrates what happens when two parties, desperate for a lot, end up in a bidding war. I could have walked out at that point but I had nothing better to do and I wanted to see how this saga ended (as if it were a box set). I Was browsing the catalogue and I noticed a property that had previously escaped my attention. It was a large Georgian 2 bedroomed mid terraced with double glazing and central heating. The real kicker was that it was just down the road from my partner's rental property that we had just renovated, so I was aware of the market in the area. The guide price was £85K and I thought, if this goes above £95K I'm out (thinking solely Refurb figures). In a bonkers move that goes against everything that our Lord and Saviour Martin Roberts (Homes Under The Hammer presenter) tells us, I didn't check out the auction pack. In my defence, I had come down with the beginnings of a serious condition called Auction Fever; potentially terminal for your wallet!

The lot came up for offer and the bidding started. It took some time to kick the bidding off but the first one came in at £80K. It crept up just as slowly and the bidding landed with a gentleman just behind me at £84K. 'Going once', my heart started beating faster, 'going twice', my heart was pounding and now my heart was metaphorically in my mouth and throbbing as my hand seemed to raise itself with a life of its own. 'We have a new bidder at £85,000'. I waited while the auctioneer appealed for a counter bid, fully expecting the gentleman behind me to come in straight away. Then the auctioneer repeated, 'going once'. . . . 'Going twice', I thought I was going to have a sceptic embolism (made up condition) . . . . 'SOLD at £85,000, a good buy that sir, please make your way to the administration desk.'

I was both ecstatic to have won and scared witless at the fact that I had not planned for this financially at all. All these courses of action I took I vehemently discourage!
But now I was bound to the sale and I told myself to walk the walk and feel good about myself. I went to the desk and paid my 10% plus buyers fee (£8,500+996) and made my way out. I briefly chatted to the auction director again who seemed pleased for me and I ran back to the car to belatedly thumb through the properties auction pack to make sure there was nothing outrageous hiding there that would prevent a mortgage company lending on it. It was all fine and so I jumped on Rightmove to confirm my valuation assessment. This was a shock. The most recent completed price was £108,000 and this was an island far off the west coast of acceptable. I panicked all the way back from the auction's Manchester location and went straight to Bredbury to see the location of the property. It was looking like I might just break even after a lot of time and effort and just renting it out; absolutely gutted. When I got to the property it was mush closer to the busy junction than I had imagined and that lowered the mood even more; what an error of judgement! In desperation I called a local agent for any glimmer of hope, praying to the

spirit of Lucy Alexander (Ex Homes presenter) as the phone rang. It worked! The agent advised me that the £108K sale had been to a family member at a large discount and I was probably looking at around the £140K mark (£5K more than I had reckoned), talk about a roller coaster ride of a day. Double pleased with myself I called up my FA and advised him that he had his work cut out. A couple of days later we got on with the mortgage application and following that I instructed my solicitor.

As I awaited progress on the mortgage application it seemed as though the product was struggling to fit and it was going to take time, too much time to get the finance through and so I was forced into the unfamiliar arena of bridging loans and auction finance. I approached a few companies who all said the same thing, my SA302s didn't stack up to their criteria and would not look at the application. I remembered that while at the auction, a member of staff that I'd worked with while working in a bank had recognised me and was touting for business. He had pointed me in the direction of an auction finance rep but he had been deep in conversation with another punter. I called the company up and explained the situation. The gentleman at Together Finance on the other line said that at his company they were more flexible about finance and accepted that SA302s don't always tell the full picture and they would look at any earnings that I could legitimately prove, including capital gains and rental income (not counted as acceptable income in the mortgage world?). I had to run around and get this all back datedly signed by an accountant which took forever and the stress of all this and the potential legal ramifications I had set myself up for were more than most people I assume could handle; but I have as much resolve as I'm required to need and that is how you need to be in the property game. Was I scared? Absolutely! But as a guest on Homes Under The Hammer replied when asked by Lucy if he was scared by his 5 X 5 bedroomed new build project, 'if you're not scared, you're not thinking big enough'; Yes son!

Everything came through just in time and I was able to complete before the deadline. This was helped by the fact that the contract and auction pack weren't sent out in a timely fashion and so I had a fair bit longer than 28 days after completion to get the job done.

It was now time to start the renovation. I had arranged a viewing shortly after the auction so I could reckon up the costs and I'd taken Walt down to give me a quote too. Remember I hadn't even viewed this house before buying it, Dion Dublin would have been turning in his grave (if not for the fact he is alive and well and presenting HUTH). It only dawned on me then that the property could have had a downstairs bathroom but luckily not only was there an upstairs bathroom; there were two of them! How the other half live eh? The property needed a full refurb and I mean a FULL refurb: re-plumbing, re-piping gas, new electrics, there was no combi boiler, the kitchen extension exterior wall was made out of wood? One of these useless bathrooms needed to be removed so as to create a double bedroom and so the soil pipe needed extending through a space where there was none. At least it had a downstairs W/C, a boarded loft and no double yellow lines outside the house and as previously mentioned uPVC double glazing. I had estimated no more than £20K to do the job but Walt said it would be £26K. It had only cost me £13K on the house around the corner so I thought this was outrageous and said that I would go this one alone and give him a shout if I came unstuck. Spoiler alert, I got very unstuck but I wanted to see this through alone because it would be excellent experience. The previous property I'd gone alone on had been almost too easy and this would be a great test. Also it would allow me to see the prices of contractors individually plus their timescales.

Side note: as you will see things had turned out differently and it transpires Walt's quote was actually fair; but I also knew that if I used Walt it would have cost me extra to put in some higher spec furnishings and there would be arguments when the builders were absent for weeks and I wanted to get this done sooner rather than later (which did not work out well at all).

Another mate of mine (builder and ex tenant, Phil) was up for doing a full refurb so I employed him and straight away he and his lads were ripping the old furniture out and getting the wallpaper stripped. Unfortunately, the polystyrene tiles on all the ceilings were so glued on, it was taking them forever. Two weeks in half the employees mutinied because they resented having to be at work at 8am???? And he lost half his work force. This along with his other responsibilities was too much and he had to withdraw from the project. I called Ciaran up to come and save my arse and he was very busy also but his mate Wayne (a time served brickie) was happy to do some labouring and also rebuild the kitchen wall. Things were looking up until Ciaran started to become conspicuously absent and acting peculiar. I haven't mentioned (as I had no reason to) that he is bi-polar and I had witnessed him lapsing on his medication before. His slow decent into anarchy led to him being hospitalised for 3 weeks and without him Wayne was a little directionless. First, I wanted to sort the now obviously leaking extension flat roof and hit mybuilder again. This did not work out well. The guys I opted for seemed the most professional but looks can be deceiving. They did a proper cowboy job with roof felt and road tar (I guess) and in the first moderate gust of wind half the roof blew off. The gutter didn't even catch any run off? My first clue should have been when they said they'd only done ¾ of it as they'd run out of board (that I'd supplied) even though Homebase was a 30 second drive away. It was only supposed to be a patch up but the leak was actually worse after they had been. So was my wallet by £750. I rang around using numbers from Google with good reviews and got a full re-roof done for £850. After arranging several contractors to come by and give me a price for the gas and plumbing work (less than half of which ever got back with a quote??) I found a good gas engineer / plumber and he put the first fix in for both. Ciaran's mate from Juliette's house renovation did a first fix and the plasterers I had used previously gave me a quote. It was a lot bigger house than my first and I was a little suspicious; so I got some others and they were still the best. They gave me a little discount and also finished off some stripping and put a stud wall up. To cut a long story short, Ciaran was released from hospital and eager to complete the job and with Wayne back on board they finished. The job lasted 5 months, which is terrible, but Walt's previous job that I haven't mentioned took that long and that's why I wanted to go it alone to a large degree. Also the final refurb cost me just under £22K not including fees.

I skipped off to the agents to get a valuation and was over the moon when they advised that we should try marketing the property at £159,999. This was top end but I thought I'd try it out. A house on the same block had been up for sale and sold for £138K. It had a downstairs shower room only and was not as high spec so everything was adding up promisingly. But then next door came on for sale at the same time at £145K and even though not as high end as mine, it still made my price look bad.

Marketing was slow for us both and we both reduced our prices to no avail. All the agents in the area said that the market had been slow and were surprised at the lack of interest in these two house. On top of this my monthly bridging loan payments had risen from £350 PCM to £790 PCM and I was beginning to get anxious and frustrated. I had borrowed the money Juliette made on hers to refurbish the place and it was holding up her progress too. So I opted for renting and remortgaging to pay off my auction finance. I opted for a 5 year fixed rate as the circumstances encouraged me to keep this property slightly longer term and interest rates were low.

I rented it out to one of the first of many viewers and went to see my FA to apply for a remortgage. Cutting to the chase, it took far longer than necessary and as a portfolio landlord the criteria for me was more stringent so my valuations had to be bob on. So of course I made sure I met up with the surveyor so as to 'altruistically' offer my sage guidance. It again worked and the figures that came back were acceptable. It valued at £150K, which is more than I'd imagined while sat at the auction and the project was satisfactorily concluded with a newly refurbished house rented out and money I owed paid back; with £26K back in the coffers.

I would like to stress that this endeavour although ending favourably, could have ended up almost ruining me temporarily and whilst I have been somewhat light hearted in its description, at times I was impulsive and reckless and only the fact that I had previous experience, some good contacts and a generous (grateful maybe) understanding partner got me through this project unscathed and on the right side (£34K in reality) of profit.

Always do your homework!

BTL Vs RENOVATE & BTL

Allow me to elucidate. My courses of action have always been one of two: buy a property to rent out or buy a property to renovate and flip. I hadn't really seen much stock in buying cheaper, renovating and not getting much profit but renting out and couldn't understand why so many people seemed keen on this play as there didn't seem to be any large immediate profit and they seemed to leave the house rented out for a couple of years and then sell which is probably where the lack of profit was made up. This would seem okay at a glance but aren't you tying up a lot of cash in this method? For someone like me who at the time was moving from one project to the next, it just wasn't viable and even if I remortgaged the house I would be getting little rent profit out of it. It was only when I was buying a house very close by that was on the market via modern method of auction that it became apparent. Now admittedly this house was on the less needier side for renovation purposes and would in fact have just about limped in to the renovation and flip category with more elbow grease from myself to make a worthwhile profit. I pondered on whether it would actually be cheaper (ie use less cash) to buy a house that was already in top notch condition and what the costs / fees involved would be and net equity sat in the property would be. Compared to buying a house that needed work but without any earth shattering profits to gain and renting it out, getting a further advance from the current lender after 6 months and totting up the resultant net equity ie which was cheaper to buy in the long run? This hinges on the fact that they are both worth the same amount of money at the end of each process. As in the actual case the first house has been bought at £125,000 and is worth £170,000 at the end. The second has just been bought for £170,000 and is in a similar condition to the first one after it has been refurbished.

So on to my favourite part - the maths:

BUY / RENOVATE / RENT / REFINANCE

Property value £125,000

Deposit at 75% LTV £31,250

Fees: purchasing solicitor £1200
  FA commission £500
  Survey free on this product but the usual is about £400
  Stamp duty £3750

Total fees: £5850

Renovation cost £15000
(it was actually £9K with lots of work myself but as the modern method of ripping me off costed £6K I have balanced the figures so the renovation fee is more realistic and there is no extortionate fee).

At the finish of this stage I had spent £52,100 cash.

With a further advance (so I didn't have to pay a fixed rate penalty remortgaging the property) where the desk top valuation agrees with £170,000, they would lend me 75% of the increase in value (on a 75% LTV product).

The increase in value is £170,000 - £125,000 (originally paid) = £45,000.

£45,000 X 75% = £33,750. (The same figure would be obtained if you remortgaged the property but you would be a couple of grand down from paying the fixed rate penalty).

So your net cash spend is the £52,100 cash paid out originally minus the £33,750 cash back ie £52,100 - £33,750 = £18,350.

Equity in property £42,500

(I have neglected the fees involved for the further advance service as they are negligible and would over complicate the maths. Also the agents rental fee would be taken out of the first months rent and is equal in both cases so cancel each other out).

BUY AND RENT OUT

Property value £170,000

Deposit at 75% LTV £42,250

Fees: purchasing solicitors £1200
 FA commission £500
 Survey £400
 Stamp duty £6000

Total fees: £8100

Total cash spent £50,350

Equity in property £42,250

To summarise you have got the same property rented out, both with the same equity left in them. In the latter case it cost you £50,350 to achieve. In the former case it cost you £18,350 to achieve (minus 6 months which the rental income of the latter property wouldn't make a dent in). So even though you have lost some of your capital you have another property on the books and you have 65% of your capital back to reinvest. This process is good to keep in mind for property that isn't quite enough to flip but there is something to be made, or you've bought to renovate and the marketing has not been quite as successful as anticipated.

FLOW CHART

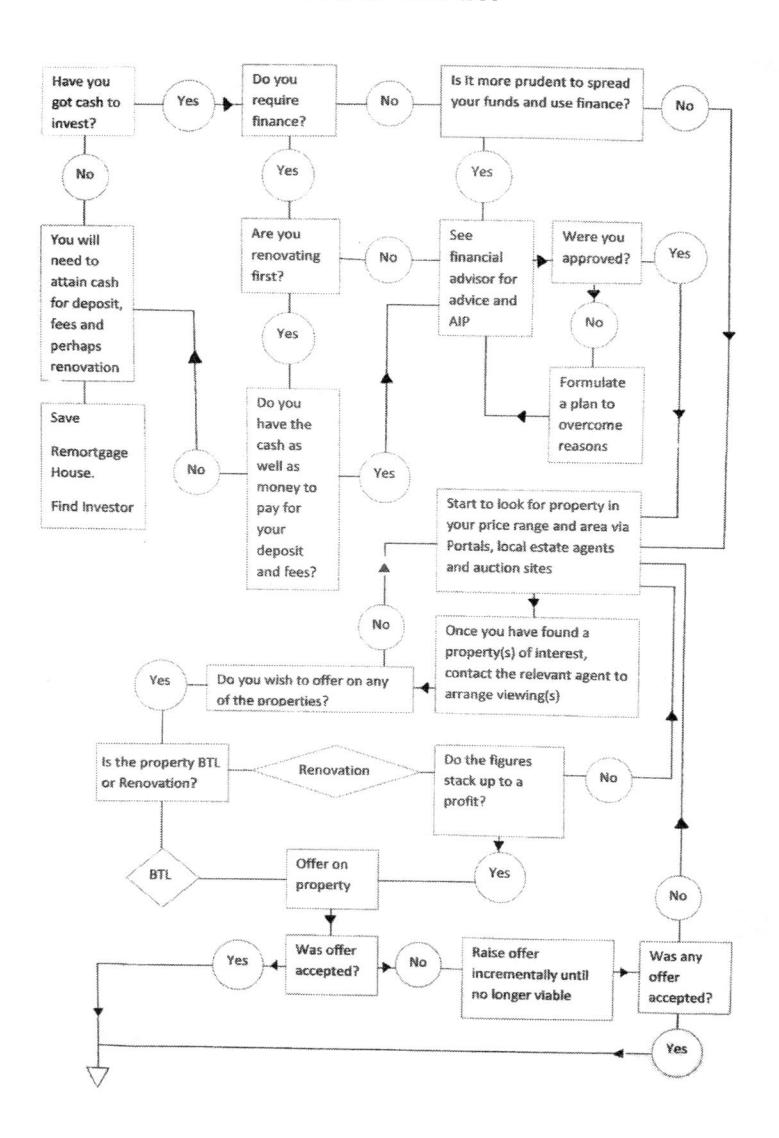

- Have you got cash to invest?
  - Yes → Do you require finance?
    - No → Is it more prudent to spread your funds and use finance?
      - No → (proceed to property search)
      - Yes → See financial advisor for advice and AIP
    - Yes → Are you renovating first?
      - No → See financial advisor for advice and AIP
      - Yes → Do you have the cash as well as money to pay for your deposit and fees?
        - No → (back to: You will need to attain cash...)
        - Yes → Start to look for property
  - No → You will need to attain cash for deposit, fees and perhaps renovation
    - Save
    - Remortgage House.
    - Find Investor

- See financial advisor for advice and AIP → Were you approved?
  - Yes → Start to look for property in your price range and area via Portals, local estate agents and auction sites
  - No → Formulate a plan to overcome reasons

- Start to look for property in your price range and area via Portals, local estate agents and auction sites → Once you have found a property(s) of interest, contact the relevant agent to arrange viewing(s) → Do you wish to offer on any of the properties?
  - No → (back to look for property)
  - Yes → Is the property BTL or Renovation?
    - Renovation → Do the figures stack up to a profit?
      - No → (back to look for property)
      - Yes → Offer on property
    - BTL → Offer on property

- Offer on property → Was offer accepted?
  - Yes → (end)
  - No → Raise offer incrementally until no longer viable → Was any offer accepted?
    - Yes → (end)
    - No → (back to look for property)

191

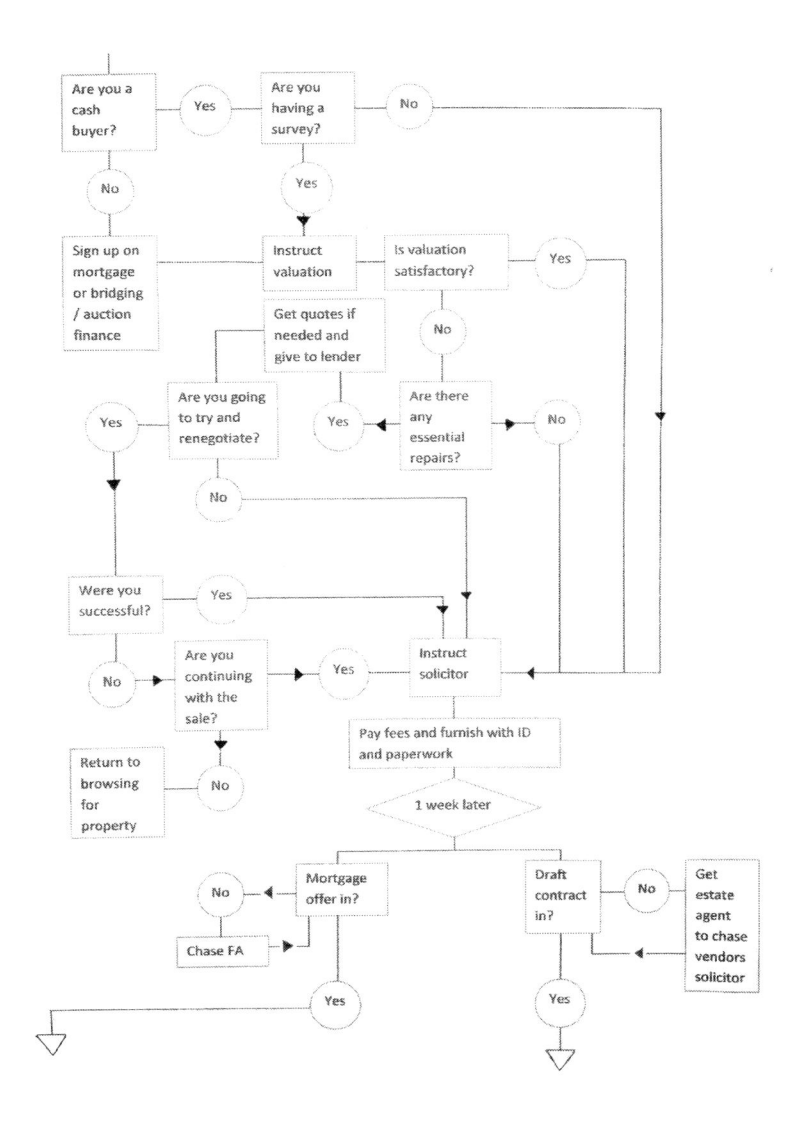

```
[Are you a cash buyer?] --Yes--> [Are you having a survey?] --No--> (to Instruct solicitor)
[Are you a cash buyer?] --No--> [Sign up on mortgage or bridging / auction finance]
[Are you having a survey?] --Yes--> [Instruct valuation]
[Sign up on mortgage or bridging / auction finance] --> [Instruct valuation]
[Instruct valuation] --> [Is valuation satisfactory?]
[Is valuation satisfactory?] --Yes--> (to Instruct solicitor)
[Is valuation satisfactory?] --No--> [Are there any essential repairs?]
[Are there any essential repairs?] --Yes--> [Get quotes if needed and give to lender] --> [Are you going to try and renegotiate?]
[Are there any essential repairs?] --No--> (to Instruct solicitor)
[Are you going to try and renegotiate?] --Yes--> [Were you successful?]
[Are you going to try and renegotiate?] --No--> (to Instruct solicitor)
[Were you successful?] --Yes--> [Instruct solicitor]
[Were you successful?] --No--> [Are you continuing with the sale?]
[Are you continuing with the sale?] --Yes--> [Instruct solicitor]
[Are you continuing with the sale?] --No--> [Return to browsing for property]
[Instruct solicitor] --> [Pay fees and furnish with ID and paperwork] --> <1 week later>
[Mortgage offer in?] --No--> [Chase FA] --> (back to Mortgage offer in?)
[Mortgage offer in?] --Yes--> ▽
[Draft contract in?] --No--> [Get estate agent to chase vendors solicitor] --> (back to Draft contract in?)
[Draft contract in?] --Yes--> ▽
```

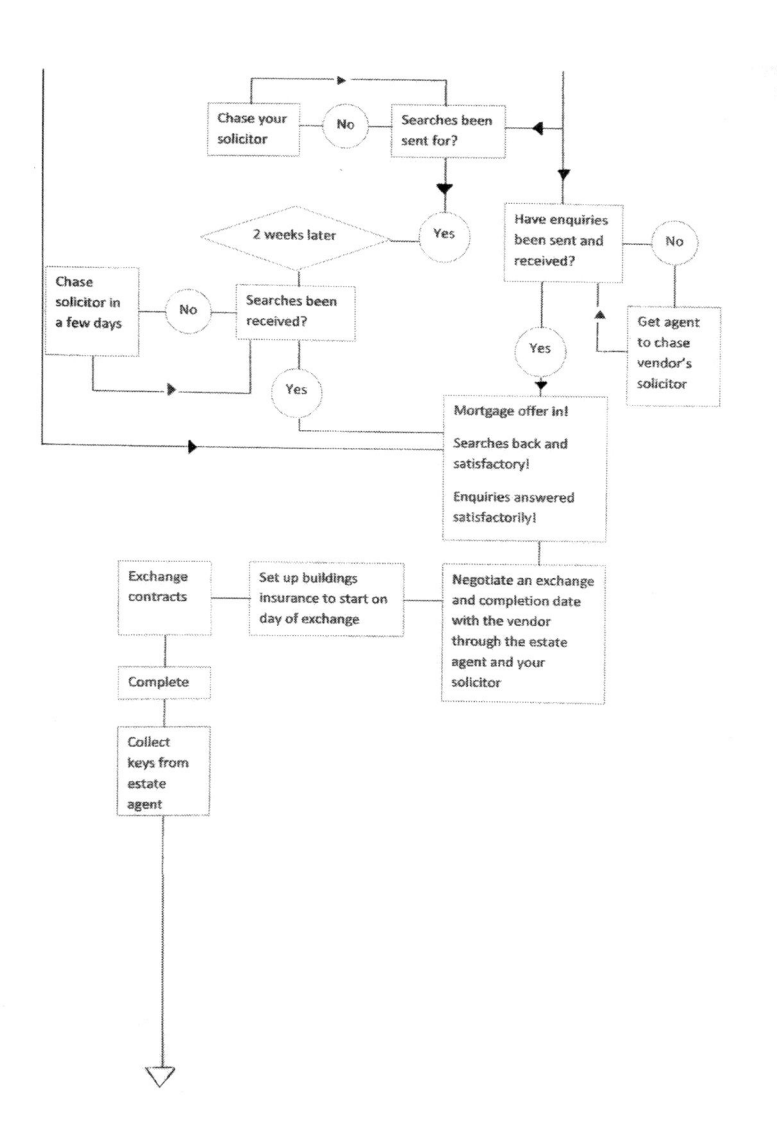

```
                              ┌──────────────┐
                              │ Searches been│◄─────────┐
          ┌──Chase your──(No)─┤  sent for?   │          │
          │  solicitor        └──────┬───────┘          │
          │                         (Yes)               │
          │                          ▼                  │
          │                    ◇ 2 weeks later ─(Yes)─  │
          │                          │                  │
┌─────────┤                         (No)                │
│ Chase   │                   ┌──────────────┐          │
│solicitor├──(No)─────────────┤Searches been │     Have enquiries      ┌──────────┐
│in a few │                   │  received?   │     been sent and ─(No)─│ Get agent│
│ days    │                   └──────┬───────┘     received?           │ to chase │
└─────────┘                        (Yes)                │              │ vendor's │
                                     │                (Yes)            │ solicitor│
                                     ▼                  │              └──────────┘
                         ┌──────────────────────┐
                         │ Mortgage offer in!   │
                         │ Searches back and    │
                         │ satisfactory!        │
                         │ Enquiries answered   │
                         │ satisfactorily!      │
                         └──────────────────────┘
```

- Exchange contracts
- Set up buildings insurance to start on day of exchange
- Negotiate an exchange and completion date with the vendor through the estate agent and your solicitor
- Complete
- Collect keys from estate agent

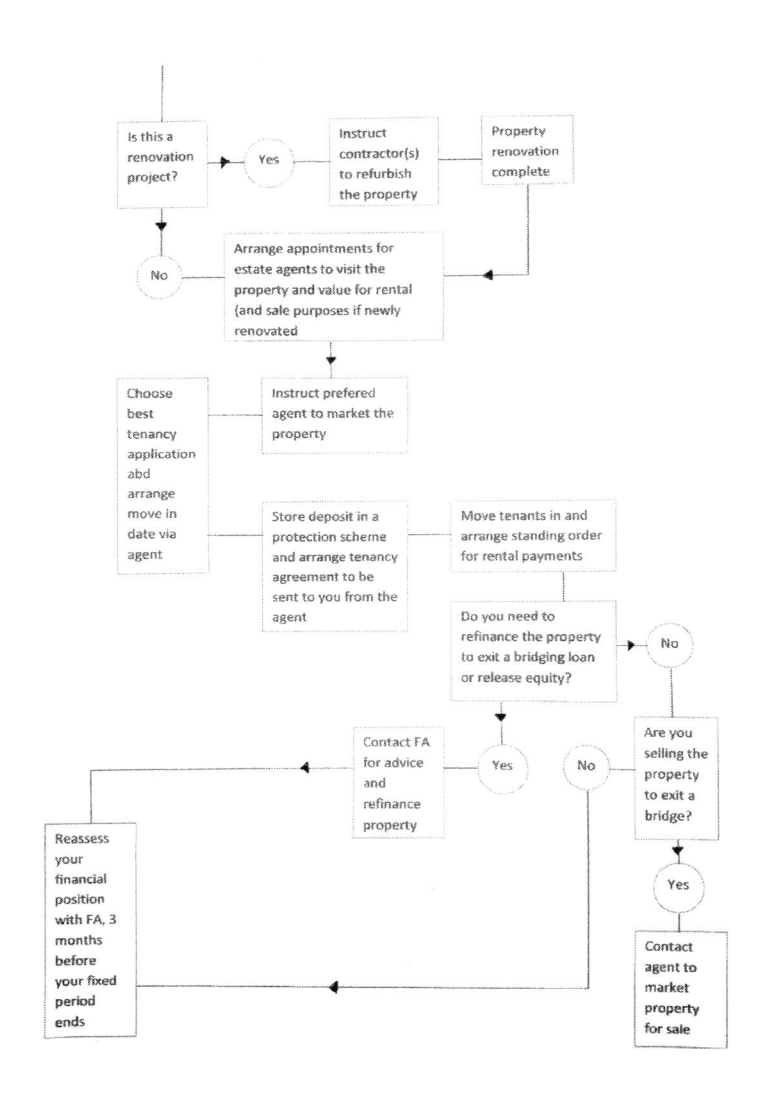

```
                    ┌─────────────┐      ┌─────────────┐      ┌─────────────┐
                    │ Is this a   │─Yes─▶│ Instruct    │─────▶│ Property    │
                    │ renovation  │      │ contractor(s)│      │ renovation  │
                    │ project?    │      │ to refurbish│      │ complete    │
                    └─────────────┘      │ the property│      └─────────────┘
                           │             └─────────────┘             │
                          No                                         │
                           ▼                                         ▼
                                     ┌──────────────────────────────────┐
                                     │ Arrange appointments for         │
                                     │ estate agents to visit the       │
                                     │ property and value for rental    │
                                     │ (and sale purposes if newly      │
                                     │ renovated                        │
                                     └──────────────────────────────────┘
```

- Is this a renovation project?
  - Yes → Instruct contractor(s) to refurbish the property → Property renovation complete → Arrange appointments for estate agents to visit the property and value for rental (and sale purposes if newly renovated)
  - No → Arrange appointments for estate agents to visit the property and value for rental (and sale purposes if newly renovated)

- Choose best tenancy application abd arrange move in date via agent ┄┄ Instruct prefered agent to market the property

- Store deposit in a protection scheme and arrange tenancy agreement to be sent to you from the agent → Move tenants in and arrange standing order for rental payments

- Do you need to refinance the property to exit a bridging loan or release equity?
  - Yes → Contact FA for advice and refinance property → Reassess your financial position with FA, 3 months before your fixed period ends
  - No → Are you selling the property to exit a bridge?
    - Yes → Contact agent to market property for sale → Reassess your financial position with FA, 3 months before your fixed period ends
    - No → Reassess your financial position with FA, 3 months before your fixed period ends

Printed in Great Britain
by Amazon